KJ

The Illustrated Lives of the Great Composers.

Verdi

Peter Southwell-Sander.
With a Foreword by Sir Geraint Evans.

Omnibus Press

London/New York/Sydney

To my mother Jackie, and my late father Geoff,
who taught me to share his love of opera

Cover design and art direction by Pearce Marchbank.
Cover photography by Gered Mankowitz, Rembrandt Bros.
Cover styled by Annie Hanson.

Printed in Great Britain by BPC Wheatons Ltd, Exeter

© Peter Southwell-Sander 1978.
First published by Midas Books in 1978.
This edition published in 1986 by Omnibus Press, a division of Book Sales Limited.

Order No. OP42365
UK ISBN 0.7119.0250.X

Exclusive Distributors:
Book Sales Limited,
8/9 Frith Street,
London W1V 5TZ
England

120 Rothschild Avenue,
Rosebery,
Sydney,
NSW 2018
Australia.

Music Sales Corporation,
257 Park Avenue South,
New York, NY10010, U.S.A.

To the Music Trade Only:
Music Sales Limited,
8/9 Frith Street,
London W1V 5TZ,
England.

Foreword

This study of Giuseppe Verdi's life and times will be welcome to all those music lovers who, through performances in opera houses, radio and television broadcasts, and gramophone records, have come to have a great affection for Verdi. Some of his works, notably *Rigoletto*, *Il trovatore*, *La traviata*, *Aida* and *Otello*, are among the world's best-known and most loved music dramas. Gradually more and more Verdi operas have been successfully introduced into the repertoire and issued on records, making us all aware of the riches to be found in his lesser-known scores.

His last opera, *Falstaff*, which in fact is considered his greatest opera, holds a special place in my own affections. I find pure enjoyment in every bar of this comic, yet tragic, masterpiece that conveys such a marvellous gusto for life.

I hope that through Peter Southwell-Sander's book many more people will come to appreciate Verdi, the background against which he composed, and his music with its never-failing fund of melody and invention.

Geraint Evans

Bibliography

Abbiati, Franco *La vita e le opere di Giuseppe Verdi* 4 vols. (Milan 1959)

Alberti, Annibale (Ed) *Verdi intimo, 1861–1886* (Verona 1931)

Budden, Julian *The Operas of Verdi* Vol. I. *From Oberto to Rigoletto* (London 1973) Vols. II and III: see Acknowledgements.

Cenzato, Giovanni *Itinerari Verdiani* (Milan 1955)

Cesari, Gaetano, and Luzio, Alessandro (Eds) *I copialettere di Giuseppe Verdi* (Milan 1913)

Crowest, Frederick *Verdi, Man and Musician* (London 1897)

Garibaldi, Luigi (Ed) *Giuseppe Verdi nelle lettere di Emmanuele Muzio ad Antonio Barezzi* (Milan 1931)

Gatti, Carlo *Verdi, the Man and his Music* trans. Elizabeth Abbott (London 1955)—[abridged version of *Verdi* 2 Vols. Milan 1931]; *Verdi nelle immagini* (Milan 1941)

Ghislanzoni, Antonio *Storia di Milano dal 1836 al 1848* (Milan 1882)

Hughes, Patric Cairns (Spike) *Famous Verdi Operas* (London 1968)

Hussey, Dyneley *Verdi* (London 1941 rev. ed. 1973)

Lumley, Benjamin *Reminiscences of the Opera* (London 1864)

Luzio, Alessandro *Carteggi Verdiani* 4 vols. (Rome 1935–1947)

Martin, George *Verdi, His Music, Life and Times* (London 1965)

Marchesi, Gustavo *Giuseppe Verdi* (Turin 1970)

Monaldi, Gino *Verdi 1839–1898* (Turin 1926)

Osborne, Charles *The Complete Operas of Verdi* (London 1969); *Letters of Giuseppe Verdi* (London 1971)

Pizzi, Italo *Per il primo sentenario della nascita di Giuseppe Verdi* (Turin 1913)

Pougin, Arthur *Giuseppe Verdi: an anecdotic history of his life and works* (trans. James Matthew, London 1887)

Rognoni, Luigi *Rossini* (Milan 1956)

Roncaglia, Gino *L'ascensione creatrice di G. Verdi* (Florence 1940. 2nd ed., 1951); *Giuseppe Verdi: L'ascensione dell' arte sua* (Naples, 1914)

Sheahan, Vincent *Orpheus at Eighty* (London 1959);

Toye, Francis *Giuseppe Verdi, his life and works* (London 1931. Reissued 1962)

Visetti, Albert *Verdi* (London 1905)

Walker, Frank *The Man Verdi* (London 1962)

'Verdi', *Grove's Dictionary of Music and Musicians*, Vol. VIII (London 1954)

Werfel, Franz and Stefan, Paul *Verdi, the man in his letters* (Vienna 1926. English trans., New York 1942)

Verdi's birthplace. A
photograph

Verdi's baptisimal entry
in the Register of the
parish church at Le
Roncole

Chapter 1
Beginnings

'Art is universal ... but it is created by individuals'—Verdi

Only five years after *Il trovatore* and *La traviata* were first performed in Italy, *The Times* correspondent, W.H. Russell, sent out to India to report on the Mutiny of 1857, visited Simla and other hill stations where English families of the Civil Service spent the summer. He found 'English bungalows, with names painted on the gateways, "Laburnham Lodge", "Prospect", "The Elms", and such-like home reminiscences and the clang of pianofortes, and streams of song rushed out through open windows, and told us that the *Traviata* had wandered here, and that the *Trovatore* could be found in every music-stand'. Such was the instant and far-reaching popularity of two of Verdi's most successful operas.

However such enthusiasm was not shared by English academics and critics who, for the first half of this century, were fairly united in giving approval only to *Otello* and *Falstaff*, while grudgingly admitting that four or five more of his operas might be profitably performed, 'opera-goers being in the main unmusical' as Sir Hubert Parry patronisingly declared. Parry, and the English musical establishment as a whole, regarded Italian music from Rossini to Puccini as a backwater compared to the mainstream of German music in general, and German opera in particular.

This was in great contrast to the situation that had existed in the seventeenth and eighteenth centuries. Italian music was then all the rage, as Mozart and Haydn, for example, discovered; they had some difficulty in obtaining posts as musical directors since every European court wanted an Italian *Kapellmeister*; both of them were required to write 'Italian' operas; and both felt a visit to Italy to be an important part of their musical education, although Haydn, like Beethoven, never achieved this ambition.

Since Italian music was no longer in such a prominent position in his lifetime, Verdi had to rise from the obscurity of a provincial tradition in order to gain the worldwide recognition he is now deservedly receiving. For Italians he had always been *Il Maestro*. Because his music not only awakened deep echoes in the soul of the Italian people, but also expressed the longings of the Risorgimento (the movement for a free and united Italy), his place in Italian music and history is profound; though even his contemporary fellow-countrymen acknowledged that he and his music did not belong to Italy alone. On the centenary of Verdi's birth in 1913, twelve years after his death, Italo Pizzi wrote:

Giuseppe Verdi's renown is part of the whole of Italy, of the whole world. One could even say of him as Manzoni said of Homer: 'He knows no homeland other than the skies.'

Yet this 'Grand Master of Italian opera' started life in humble surroundings. His birthplace in the tiny village of Le Roncole in the north of Italy was a simple tavern with roughly-timbered floors and ceilings, a long sloping roof enclosing a stable on one side, and shuttered windows looking out onto the flat, dull plain of Parma. The house still stands and is maintained by the Italian government as a national monument.

Early biographers stated that Verdi's parents were illiterate peasants, an image certainly fostered by the composer himself, who wrote towards the end of his life: 'Alas! Born poor in a poor village I had no way to teach myself anything. They put a miserable spinet under my hands, and some time later I began to write notes ... notes upon notes ... that is all!' In fact, both his parents came from families of small landowners, innkeepers and grocers, who could not strictly be called peasants. Recent research has shown that Carlo, Verdi's father, could not have been illiterate since he was secretary of the treasury of St Michele Arcangelo in Le Roncole for fifteen years. His father, Verdi's grandfather, had moved from Sant' Agata where six generations of the family had lived to Le Roncole where Carlo, born in 1785, kept the village *osteria* (inn).

On 30 January 1805 he married Luigia Uttini, a publican's daughter from Piacenza. Their son, Giuseppe Fortunino Francesco, was born on 10 October 1813: a year notable in literature for the publication of Jane Austen's *Pride and Prejudice* and Shelley's *Queen Mab*; a year that saw the

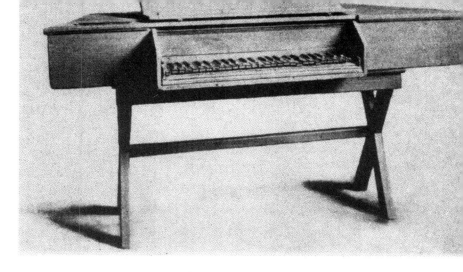

Verdi's spinet (Milan, La Scala Museum)

composition of Schubert's First Symphony and the first performance in Vienna of Beethoven's Seventh Symphony; a year in which Rossini's *Tancredi* and *L'Italiana in Algeri* were first triumphantly performed; and a year, finally, poised on the brink of great social change—Stephenson used the first effective steam locomotive in 1814, and by 1820 iron steamships and transatlantic steamers had made their appearance.

The day after his birth, Verdi was baptised in the parish church where his name is recorded in Latin. His mother mistakenly told him that he was born on the 9th, which he always celebrated as his birthday even after discovering the error when he was sixty-three. Carlo Verdi had to walk to the neighbouring town of Busseto to register the birth in French as 'Joseph Fortunin François' since Napoleon's army had occupied Northern Italy from the turn of the century.

When Verdi was less than a year old, Napoleon abdicated at Fontainbleau and the combined armies of Austria and Russia drove the French out of Italy. Although many fanciful and totally untrue anecdotes have been told about Verdi, there is some reason to believe the story recounted by his second wife to a friend, from which one may conclude that Verdi himself believed it to be true. Some Russian soldiers passed through Le Roncole, looting, raping and killing some of the inhabitants, but Verdi's mother saved herself and her baby by hiding in the church belfry. Apart from their composer son, Carlo and Luigia Verdi had one daughter, Giuseppa Francesca, who was mentally-retarded as a result of meningitis. Two and a half years younger than her brother, she died at Le Roncole in 1833 when she was only seventeen.

11

The castle at Busseto.
Painting by Bottini

The village church of Madonna dei Prati was an important influence in Verdi's early years; but it was the music, and not the Catholic faith, that touched the boy. Boito, his last and greatest librettist, wrote of him: 'He lost his belief early, like all of us, but he retained, more than the rest of us perhaps, a regret for it all his life.' He was taught to read and write by the local priest, and his first music master was the village organist, Pietro Baistrocchi. He obviously showed early talent, for when he was eight, his father brought him a spinet, which does not appear to have been quite so 'miserable' as he later maintained. It was repaired free by a neighbour, Stefano Cavaletti 'seeing the good disposition the young Verdi has for learning to play this instrument, which is sufficient for my complete satisfaction'. He always treasured this instrument, and it is now preserved in the La Scala Museum.

Soon both priest and organist died, so at the age of ten Giuseppe went to the *ginnasio* (the grammar school) in Busseto, obtaining lodgings with a cobbler, and walking the three miles back to Le Roncole on Sundays and feast days to play the organ for a salary of thirty-six lire per annum. (Thirteen years later he was to turn down the post of cathedral organist of Monza at eight times that salary). He often carried his boots on the walk in order not to wear them out, and once, on a Christmas morning, fell into a deep irrigation ditch beside the road from which he was saved from drowning by a passing peasant.

He was extremely fortunate in meeting in Busseto the man from whom his father purchased wine, the merchant Antonio Barezzi. Known locally as a *maniaco dilettante*, he was an enthusiastic amateur flautist who could turn his hand to play several other instruments. He had founded the Busseto Philharmonic Society, which rehearsed and performed in his house on the *piazza* at the end of the main street of the sleepy little town: consequently he took a great interest in the budding composer, showing him every kindness. Verdi now studied for four years with Ferdinando Provesi, choirmaster and organist of the collegiate church of San Bartolomeo and director of Barezzi's Philharmonic Society. In 1829, having failed to obtain the post of organist at nearby Soragna, the sixteen-year old Verdi began to deputize for his teacher as organist in Busseto, while continuing to play at Le Roncole.

Margherita Barezzi (1814–40). Portrait in oils by A. Mussini (Milan, La Scala Museum)

Milan, the Corso di Porta. Copperplate engraving by L. Cherbuin

His other musical activities were numerous and varied: teaching younger pupils, copying parts for the Philharmonic Society, directing rehearsals, playing the piano at Barezzi's musical gatherings, and composing. He recalled later:

From my thirteenth year to my eighteenth year (the age at which I went to Milan to study counterpoint) I wrote an assortment of pieces: marches for brass band by the hundred, perhaps as many little *sinfonie*, that were used in church, in the theatre or at concerts, five or six concertos and sets of variations for the pianoforte, which I played myself at concerts, many serenades, cantatas (arias, duets, very many trios) and various pieces of church music of which I remember only a *Stabat Mater*.

When a visiting company performed Rossini's *Il barbiere di Siviglia* at the Busseto theatre in 1828 (the year of Schubert's death following Beethoven's during the previous year), Verdi scored a great success with an overture he wrote for it. A cantata of this period *I deliri di Saul* was much praised, but **Verdi later tried to suppress all works written in his youth,** although some have survived.

Barezzi became more and more like a father to his young protégé so that in May 1831 Verdi left his lodgings and moved into Barezzi's house. The merchant had two sons and four daughters, the eldest of whom, Margherita, took singing and piano lessons from Verdi. When it became apparent that they had fallen in love, Barezzi, wanting to do his best for his future son-in-law, decided that he must continue his studies in Milan, for Busseto could teach him no more. Carlo Verdi was persuaded to apply for a grant for his son from the Monte di Pietà e d'Abbondanza, a charitable institution formed in Busseto in the seventeenth century to assist poor children. Verdi was awarded a grant to start in November 1833, which meant that Barezzi had to support him for the first year of his studies. Verdi moved to Milan, taking lodgings with the nephew of Pietro Seletti, the priest who had taught him in Busseto. One contemporary account of Milan is given by an Englishman, Samuel Rogers, in his *Italian Journal (1814–1821)*:

> The narrow streets, the houses of a pearly-white, the balcony to every window from which a female figure is almost always looking as in P[aulo] Veronese and Tintoret[to], the open turrets on the roofs, and the statues on the churches and palaces all give one back what I have so often seen with pleasure in Italian paintings.

Such a romantic view was not shared by Antonio Ghislanzoni who visited Milan in 1836. He described pavements crossed by open sewers, crowded back-street dwellings, and dingy streets frequented by drunkards, thieves

Milan Cathedral, the greatest example of Gothic architecture in Italy (Mary Evans)

and whores. The signs of poverty and squalor were everywhere. Houses of ill-repute from which prostitutes solicited from doors and windows were to be found even in the city centre near the cathedral. 'Above the customary shouting, the cracking of whips, the noisy games of *mora* in the *osterie*, were heard from numerous slaughter-houses the dying groans and squeals of calves and pigs.' Rogers was quite delighted by the cathedral with its wall-painting of *The Last*

15

Supper by Leonardo da Vinci; Ghislanzoni found that this cathedral was used as a public urinal as well as a centre for the black market at night.

In June Verdi applied to be admitted as a paying pupil at the Milan Conservatory. After a brief examination he was turned down. He never forgot this, and years later, when the members of the Conservatory wanted to re-name it after him, he refused commenting: 'They wouldn't have me young. They cannot have me old.' In fact, he was turned down for perfectly sound reasons. The Conservatory was crowded to capacity; there was only one piano for the use of all pianoforte pupils; Verdi was a 'foreigner' in Lombardy-Venetia; he was four years over the maximum age for entrance; and 'Signor Angeleri, teacher of the pianoforte, found that the said Verdi would have need to change the position of his hand, which, he said, at the age of eighteen would be difficult'. The examiners were, however, encouraging about his composition. The registrar, Basily, commented:

As regards the composition that he presented as his own, I am in complete agreement with Signor Piantanida, teacher of counterpoint and vice-registrar, that if he (Verdi) applies himself attentively and patiently to study the rules of counterpoint, he will be able to control the genuine imagination he shows himself to possess, and thus turn out creditably as a composer.

Another of the examiners, Alessandro Rolla, a conductor at La Scala, advised Verdi: 'Give up all idea of the Conservatory; choose a teacher in the city; I suggest either Lavigna or Negri.'

So for the next three years Verdi studied under Vincenzo Lavigna, La Scala's *maestro al cembalo* (accompanist and director of music). 'In the three years I spent with him I did nothing but study canons and fugues ... Nobody taught me orchestration or dramatic technique.' Barezzi not only paid for his lessons, music, board and lodgings—all of which amounted to nearly four times the grant from the Monte di Pietà—he also bought him a season ticket to La Scala on Lavigna's advice and gave him a square piano (now in the La Scala Museum).

After Verdi had been studying for a year in Milan, his first music-teacher, Provesi, died, leaving vacant the combined position of *maestro di cappella*-cum-organist at the church, and municipal music master of Busseto. With no money to attend Provesi's funeral (nor the funeral of his own sister who died a month later), Verdi remained studying in Milan. Barezzi and the Philharmonic Society naturally wanted him to succeed

Alessandro Rolla (1757–1841). Between 1782 and 1802 he led the orchestra at Parma, and then went to Milan as leader and conductor of the opera at La Scala. He became professor of composition at Milan Conservatoire in 1805. It was while Rolla was at Parma that Paganini, one of the greatest violinists of the Romantic age, took some lessons with him

Provesi, but Lavigna made it quite clear that his pupil needed a further year's tuition. Meanwhile the ecclesiastical authorities nominated their own candidate, a local choirmaster, Giovanni Ferrari, although for some undiscovered reason they did not appoint him until nearly a year later in June 1834, setting aside Verdi's belated application sent in at Barezzi's urgent request.

A bitter local feud began: the members of the Philharmonic Society invaded the church, seizing the music so that Ferrari could not use it; 'there were brawls in the streets, lampoons, arrests, prosecutions' as the two sides fought each other: Verdi conducted Philharmonic band concerts at the same time as Ferrari was playing in the church. Eventually the government of Parma confirmed Ferrari's appointment as organist of San Bartolemeo, but declared that a competition must be held for the post of *maestro di musica*. A royal decree banned the use of instrumental music in the church to prevent further outrages, and this edict was to remain in force for seventeen years until Verdi himself succeeded in having it rescinded in 1852.

La Scala, Milan.
Painting by A. Inganni,
1852 (Milan, La Scala
Museum)

During this dispute, Verdi had a stroke of good fortune. He attended the Milan Philharmonic Society's rehearsals of Haydn's *Creation*, and on one occasion none of the three conductors appeared, so Pietro Massini, the director, asked him to take their place. He accompanied and conducted with such aplomb that he was entrusted with the public performance, which was so successful that it had to be repeated before the Archduke and Milanese high society.

Meanwhile the musical wars raged in Busseto. Wearied by them, Verdi enlisted Lavigna's assistance in applying for the position of organist at Monza cathedral at an annual salary of nearly 3,000 lire (Busseto were offering 657 lire per annum). The Philharmonic Society promptly reminded him of the benefits he had received from his own town, even threatening to restrain him by force if he tried to leave. He complained to Lavigna:

If my benefactor Barezzi would not have had to suffer on my account the almost general hostility of the district, I should have left straight away; neither their reproaches about benefits nor their

18

menaces would have been able to affect me. Even if I did receive from the Monte di Pietà a slender pension towards my support in Milan, this benefit ought not to purchase my degradation and slavery, or I should be constrained to consider the said benefit no longer a generous act, but a mean one.

Verdi was examined at Parma by Giuseppe Alinovi, the court organist, after Ferrari had withdrawn from the competition. The old man told the twenty-two year old Verdi: 'You have enough knowledge to be *maestro* in Paris or London, rather than in Busseto. I confess that I should not have been able to do in a whole day what you have done in a few hours.'

In April 1836 he received his contract as *maestro di musica* of Busseto and became engaged to Margherita, whom he married on 4 May. Of Margherita little is known. No love-letters between them survive, for Verdi shielded his private life from public gaze, with the result that many early biographies were highly speculative. (However from 1844 he kept copies [*I copialettere*] of much of his business correspondence with conductors, publishers, librettists, impresarios and the like, although these are by no means complete; in addition many other letters remain scattered in museums and private collections all over Italy.)

After Verdi's success conducting Haydn's *Creation* (and later a performance of Rossini's *La Cenerentola*), Massini suggested the idea of writing an opera for Milan's Teatro Filodrammatico. Returning in 1838 to Busseto to take up his post as *maestro di musica*, Verdi worked on an opera until he left Busseto in 1839. There is little doubt that he first worked on a libretto *Rocester* by Antonio Piazza but that, after he failed to have it performed in Parma, he re-worked parts of it into *Oberto, Conte di San Bonifacio*. This seems to be proved by the recent discovery that the autograph score of the Act II quartet in *Oberto* had the name 'Rocester' crossed out and 'Riccardo' superimposed. *Rocester* itself was never performed and is now lost. The projected performance of *Oberto* at Milan did not take place, but two famous singers, Giuseppina Strepponi and Giorgio Ronconi, liked the music enough to persuade the Milan impresario Merelli that he should obtain it for La Scala. The *première* on 17 November 1839 was a distinct success with Ignazio Marini in the title-rôle, so Merelli gave the composer a contract to write three operas in the next two years.

Meanwhile Margherita had given birth to two children, Virginia and Icilio, but tragically they died within fourteen months of each other—both were little more than a year old.

Antonio Barezzi, Verdi's father-in-law. Oil painting in the Barezzi house, Busseto

Felice Romani (1780–1865). Drawing by P. Bizzato

Worse was to come. Antonio Barezzi recorded in his diary in June 1840: 'In Milan at midday on the feast of Corpus Christi my beloved daughter Margherita died in my arms of some terrible disease perhaps unknown to medical science, [in fact it was encephalitis] she was in the flower of her years and at the height of her good fortune, for she had become the lifelong companion of that excellent young man Giuseppe Verdi, *maestro di musica*.' Heart-broken, Verdi returned to Busseto, asking Merelli to release him from his contract. Merelli refused, so after a few months Verdi returned to Milan 'in the midst of terrible sorrow to compose and see through to its production a comic opera'.

The effect on him of the deaths of his wife and children within two years is hard to assess. Years afterwards he incorrectly stated that they all died within three months of each other; such a mistake surely shows how these bereavements became etched on his memory as a single and terrible tragedy. Small wonder that he did not write another comic opera until *Falstaff* fifty years later.

Disaster followed disaster. *Un giorno di regno* (*King for a day*) was produced in August 1840; hissed by the public, condemned by the critics, the second performance was cancelled. The libretto by Felice Romani was based on the story of King Stanislas Lescinski of Poland who travelled to Warsaw disguised as a coachman, while a young French officer impersonated him. But it was a libretto full of difficulties and unanswered questions, which Verdi was apparently too depressed or hurried to have altered. Much of the music is monotonous and derivative recalling Rossini and Donizetti, yet it does have joyful and lyrical moments that may account for its later success in Naples and Venice during Verdi's lifetime.

Nevertheless this failure following his personal tragedy depressed him utterly. He later recalled: '*Un giorno di regno* failed to please: certainly the music was partly to blame, but partly, too, the performance. With mind tormented by my domestic misfortunes, embittered by the failure of my work, I was convinced that I could find no consolation in my art and decided never to compose again.' He gave up thinking about music, taking rooms in Milan where he nursed his bitterness.

Chapter 2
SUCCESS

'The only one among us capable of writing Grand Opera'—Rossini

It is possible that Verdi might have vanished into obscurity after these set-backs, but one winter evening he came across Merelli in the street, a chance meeting that was to lead to the turning-point of his musical career. Bartolomeo Merelli had begun to work in the theatre as a librettist, including a collaboration with his friend Donizetti; but while still in his teens he became a theatrical agent. Bellini reported that he had the reputation of being a swindler; the German composer Nicolai called him 'a scoundrel, and already known as such in the whole of Italy'; nevertheless Merelli gradually improved his position and in 1836 was appointed not only joint lessee of the Kärntnertor theatre in Vienna, but also impresario of La Scala, Milan. To the almost unknown Verdi he was generous and kind. At their encounter he did not remind the young composer that he was still under contract to produce two more operas, but spoke rather of his own difficulties. Needing a new opera to present, he had given a libretto by Solera to Nicolai, who had turned it down. Nicolai later explained: 'I had to refuse, convinced that interminable raging, blood-shedding, reviling, striking, and murdering was no subject for me.' Later, in 1879, Verdi recounted to Giulio Ricordi what happened next:

'Imagine!' said Merelli 'A libretto by Solera! Stupendous! Magnificent! Extraordinary! Effective, grandiose,dramatic situations and beautiful verses! But the pig-headed composer won't hear of it and says it's a hopeless libretto. I'm at my wits end to know where to find another one quickly.'

Taking Verdi to the theatre, Merelli gave him Solera's libretto, asking him to take it home to read.

On my way [Verdi recalled], I felt a kind of indefinable malaise, a very deep sadness, a distress that filled my heart. I got home and with

Bartolomeo Merelli (1793–1879). Oil painting

Verdi in 1842 at the time of *Nabucco*. Drawing by G. Trucchi

an almost violent gesture threw the manuscript on the table, standing upright in front of it. The book had opened in falling on the table; without knowing how, I gazed at the page that lay before me; and read this line:

'Va, pensiero, sull'ali dorate'

I ran through the verses that followed and was much moved, all the more because they were almost a paraphrase from the Bible, the reading of which had always delighted me.

I read one passage, then another. Then resolute in my determination to write no more, I forced myself to close the booklet and went to bed. But it was no use—I couldn't get *Nabucco* out of my head. Unable to sleep, I got up and read the libretto, not once, but two or three times, so that by morning I knew Solera's libretto by heart.

Merelli's stratagem had almost worked, though Verdi was still resolved not to compose any more and next morning took the manuscript back to the theatre. The impresario would have none of it.

'Isn't it beautiful?' he said to me.
'Very beautiful!'
'Well then—set it to music!'
'I wouldn't dream of it. I won't hear of it.'
'Set it to music! Set it to music!'
And so saying he took the libretto, thrust it into my overcoat pocket, took me by the shoulders and not only pushed me out of the room but locked the door in my face.

Verdi's own accounts differ as to whether he immediately set to work on the score or left it untouched for several months. What is certain is that in the autumn of 1841 he presented the finished score to Merelli, reminding him that he had promised to perform a new opera if given two months' notice before the new season. Merelli was however already committed to three other new operas by established composers, so could not risk a fourth by a beginner in the same season. *Nabucco* would have to wait until the spring. The *cartelloni* (the La Scala posters) went up in the streets of Milan without announcing Verdi's opera.

The assistance of patrons and friends may have been helpful, even necessary, previously; now the twenty-eight year old Verdi needed all his own determination and conviction. There is no doubt he had both. (For example, he had already locked Solera in his room, refusing to let him out until he had replaced a love duet which he did not like 'as it held up the action and seemed to me to detract somewhat from the Biblical grandeur of the drama'. Solera, who had a violent

Giuseppina Strepponi
(1815–97) with the score
of *Nabucco*, 1842

temper, disliked such treatment, but suddenly sat down and in a quarter of an hour wrote the prophecy of Zaccaria.) It was crucial that Verdi now stood up to Merelli in the same way, so **he wrote him a strongly-worded letter. The impresario** eventually capitulated, possibly after pressure from the singers Giuseppina Strepponi and Giorgio Ronconi (who were to be the first Abigaille and Nabucco), on condition that existing scenery and costumes from a ballet on the same subject given four years previously could be used to save expense. Fresh *cartelloni* announced: *Nabuccodonosor* (the original title was later dropped in favour of the easier *Nabucco*).

The opera was first triumphantly performed on 9 March 1842. 'With this opera my artistic career may be said to have begun.' The first-night audience greeted it with wild enthusiasm, encoring the third act chorus 'Va, pensiero, sull'ali dorate' ('Fly, thought, on wings of gold'), the words of which had originally captured the composer's own imagination. Since encores were often turned into anti-

The interior of La Scala, Milan, where *Nabucco* was first performed on 9 March 1842. Lithograph by Rupp

Austrian demonstrations, they were forbidden by law. This chorus, central to the opera, so melodic and memorable with its surging tune, turned Verdi overnight into a famous composer who had expressed in his music the nationalistic fervour of the Risorgimento.

The Milanese could at once identify with the oppressed Jews under the Babylonian rule of Nebuchadnezzar as they sang of their longing for their homeland and freedom:

'Oh, mia patria si bella e perduta!
Oh, membranza si cara e fatal!'
('Oh, my country so lovely and lost!
Oh, remembrance so dear and so fraught with doom!')

The audience responded to that chorus not because they were cut off from their homeland, but because they longed for it to be re-born as a united country. In the previous century Italy had been composed of many states, namely three kingdoms (Sardinia, Naples and Sicily), three ancient republics (Venice, Genoa and Lucca), the Papal States and various duchies. Yet even these states were not independent, for the foreign rule of the Austrian Habsburgs had replaced that of the Spanish branch of the same family at the end of the seventeenth century; furthermore by 1808 the French under Napoleon had captured all the Italian mainland.

While Verdi was still a baby, the French in their turn were driven out of Italy and by the Treaty of Vienna in 1815 most of the duchies and kingdoms, though reduced in number, were

Napoleon's Triumphal Entry into Milan. Napoleon, on defeating the Austrians, created Milan capital of the Cisalpine Republic in 1797 and then capital of the Kingdom of Italy (1805–14). Engraving (Mary Evans)

restored to their respective rulers, with Austrian government re-established in much of the country. Parma, Verdi's homeland, was now ruled by Marie-Louise, Napoleon's second wife and daughter of the Austrian Emperor. Many in Italy had had great hopes that Napoleon's kingdom of Italy would be truly democratic and united, but the pattern of events in France repeated themselves on Italian soil. Anarchy and injustice, the plundering of Italy's cultural treasures to enrich the Louvre, the new republics that turned out to be democratic only in name, all added fuel to the flames of Italian longing for true freedom.

The Holy Alliance of Russia, Austria and Prussia was now fixed on a course of conservative reaction to the revolutionary movement that had been spreading throughout Europe. The Austrian Chancellor Metternich therefore avowed that he would 'extinguish the spirit of Italian unity and ideas about constitutions'. Verdi's nationalistic operas gave the audience a chance to express these longings in public demonstrations.

Verdi's publisher, Giovanni Ricordi (1785–1853), founder of the Milanese publishing house that still bears his name. The business was taken over subsequently by his son, Tito Ricordi (1811–88), and then his grandson, Giulio (1840–1912). Engraving by Bignoli

Cavaliere Andrea Maffei (1798–1885). An old photograph

Since large public gatherings were otherwise illegal, the opera houses at this time were, along with the cafés, one of the main meeting places of Italian life. Food and drink were served in the long intermissions, during which opera-goers talked business and politics. Just as it would be wrong to think of the Risorgimento as a national movement reaching all Italians, so it would be equally wrong to overlook the fact that the majority of people caught up in this new 'spirit of the age' were the intelligentsia—those, in other words, who made up the greater part of opera audiences. There is no evidence to suggest that Solera or Verdi consciously set out to stir up nationalistic fervour in *Nabucco*, although there is no doubt that Verdi's sympathies were with the national liberal movement.

When the publisher Giovanni Ricordi saw that *Nabucco* was a success, he printed the vocal score with a title page proclaiming: 'Set into music and humbly dedicated to H.R.H. the Most Serene Archduchess Adelaide of Austria, 31 March 1842, by Giuseppe Verdi.' At first sight it may seem strange that an opera which had already been so identified with the cause of a free Italy was dedicated to a member of the ruling Austrian family. One must remember, however, that in the first place Verdi was only at the start of his career and had not composed his most 'subversive' operas; and secondly, although the Archduchess was a cousin to the Austrian Emperor, she had lived all her life in Milan where her father was one of the more popular Austrian officials. Verdi's dedication proved to be most aptly chosen, for a month after publication of the score she married the Duke of Savoy, Vittorio Emanuele, who was to become the first King of Italy eighteen years later, while both her son and grandson became Kings of Italy during Verdi's lifetime.

The success of *Nabucco* opened many doors to its composer since everyone wished to be the friend of the now famous man. One of the lasting friendships he made at this time was with the poet Cavaliere Andrea Maffei and his wife, Clarina, who ran Milan's most sparkling salon. Such salons were the meeting-places for the city's 'society' and were held in private houses. Contessa Maffei's salon reflected her husband's literary taste and her own interest in politics, for she was a convinced supporter of the Risorgimento. She had 'an open and enthusiastic affection for people' and could certainly hold her own in political discussion with the men she entertained in her salon, which for fifty years was such a focal point of

Contessa Clara (Clarina) Maffei (1814–86)

Milanese life that it is still commemorated by a plaque on the house. Through it the young composer from the country broadened his experience by meeting many important figures of Italian life.

Contessa Maffei was sixteen years younger than her husband, being only twenty-eight when Verdi first met them in 1842. Their marriage however was not happy; Andrea lived by the maxim of the Venetian playwright, Goldoni: 'La mattina una messetta, l'apodisnar una bassetta, la sera una donnetta' ('A quick mass in the morning, a little flutter at cards in the afternoon, a bit of dalliance in the evening'). Unlike his wife's affaire with Carlo Tenca, the editor of a well-known periodical, which was accepted by Milanese society because of the obvious affection of the pair, the Cavaliere's affaires and gambling became a scandal, so that the couple separated in 1846. Verdi witnessed the separation agreement but remained a lifelong friend of both. He set three of Andrea's songs in a collection published in 1845, and enlisted

Vincenzo Bellini (1801–35). In a letter to Camille Bellaigue, 2 May 1898, Verdi wrote: 'Bellini is weak instrumentally and harmonically, it's true, but he is rich in feeling, and in a certain personal melancholy, which is completely his own. Even in his less well-known operas ... there are long, long, long spun-out melodies, like nothing that has been written before.' Engraving by Focosi

his help with the text of *Macbeth*. Later Maffei was to provide the libretto for another of Verdi's operas, *I masnadieri*. The Contessa became Verdi's confidante and his surviving letters to her reveal many of the trials and tribulations of his artistic career.

Another salon to which Verdi soon gained access was that of Giuseppina Appiani, which had a strong musical bias since she cultivated in succession three of Italy's leading composers—Bellini, Donizetti and Verdi. Bellini had written *La sonnambula* in her house, and Donizetti composed *Linda di Chamounix* there. Shortly after hearing *Nabucco*, however, Donizetti left Milan for Bologna (and on the journey was heard to exclaim to himself: 'Oh, that *Nabucco*! Beautiful! Beautiful! Beautiful!'). Mme Appiani at once felt freer to secure Verdi for her salon without offending the senior composer. It was once thought that she might have had one, or indeed all, of these composers, as her lover, but early biographers had confused her with another lady of the same name and consequently thought her to be much younger than she really was. There is no evidence to suggest that she was ever Verdi's mistress.

After the success of *Nabucco*, Merelli immediately

Temistocle Solera (1815–78), the librettist of *Nabucco*, *I Lombardi*, *Giovanna d'Arco* and *Attila* who worked with Verdi between 1841 and 1846. An old photograph

commissioned Verdi to write the *opera d'obbligo* for the Carnival season. (A great deal of public attention always centred on this obligatory opera and it was a considerable compliment for a composer to be asked to write it.) So well had the impresario profited from *Nabucco* that he now had a set of luxury apartments in Milan, a magnificent country villa with a stable of sixteen English horses and a fine art collection. He could afford to be magnanimous and asked Verdi to name his own fee for the next opera. Verdi consulted Giuseppina Strepponi, who had already helped him so much and who was later to play such an important part in his life as his companion and second wife. The *prima donna* suggested that he should ask the same as Bellini had received for *Norma* eleven years earlier, and this was agreed.

Verdi chose another theme likely to stir the Italian audiences' aspirations and imagination in Tomasso Grossi's epic poem *I Lombardi alla Prima Crociata* (*The Lombards on the First Crusade*). Once again the librettist was Temistocle Solera. His life had already been somewhat highly-coloured: son of an imprisoned Italian patriot, he ran away from school in Vienna to join a circus, where he is said to have enjoyed the 'ripe favours' of the manager's wife when he was only thirteen. He was recaptured by the police in Budapest and returned to Milan where he commenced writing poetry and operas; two of his operas were given at La Scala by the time he was twenty-four, no mean achievement even in those days.

The political overtones of *Nabucco* were probably instinctive, perhaps even accidental. In *I Lombardi* nationalistic fervour is much more evident, especially in the song of the crusaders in the last Act's 'O Signore, dal tetto natio' ('O Lord, from the home of our birth'), in which they pray for water in the desert far away from 'the fair brooklets of Lombardy's fields'. People in the first-night audience felt a strong affinity with the crusading Lombards defending their Holy Land against the Saracens, whom they naturally identified as the Austrians. Although the police tried to enforce the no-encores ruling, it was broken many times and when the Lombards cried out 'La Santa Terra oggi nostra sarà' ('Today the Holy Land will be ours') many shouted 'Si' and cheered wildly. The first-night was on 11 February 1843, just over a month after the *premières* of *Der fliegende Holländer*, by Verdi's exact contemporary Wagner in Dresden, and Donizetti's *Don Pasquale* in Paris.

In the future Verdi was to have many problems with the political censor, now fully alerted by the public demonstrations that marked performances of *Nabucco* and *I*

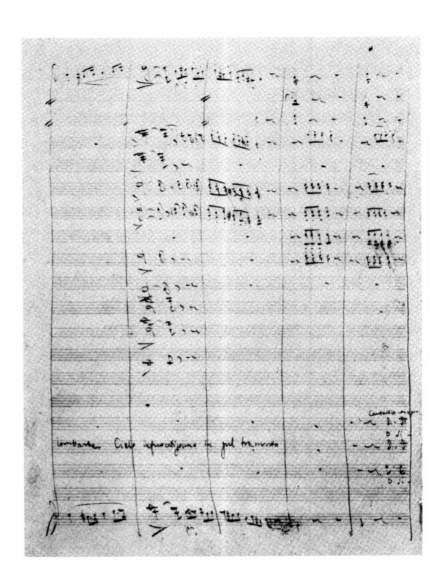

'O Signore, dal tetto natio', *I Lombardi*, Act IV, sc. iii. Autograph page (G. Ricordi & Co.)

Lombardi. Surprisingly it was not politics, but religion, that caused the censorship difficulties during the rehearsal period of *I Lombardi*. The Archbishop of Milan, having discovered that the text contained the representation of a baptism and other matters he considered to be sacrilegious, demanded that the police investigate. In spite of Verdi's protestations that he would alter nothing, Merelli and Solera had to appear before the Chief of Police, Torresani, who, being a music-lover, insisted only that the words *Ave Maria* be changed to *Salve Maria*. This minor change allowed him to reassure the Archbishop that the offending material had been dealt with!

The critics were more cautious than the audience in their

appraisal of *I Lombardi* and indeed, although it was initially as popular as *Nabucco*, it did not have the same continuing success. This must be due partly to the fragmentary nature of the libretto (four main sections in eleven scenes), also partly because of the uneven score. Some of the music is trivial and banal; yet there are what Boito was to speak of as 'marvellous traces, here and there, of eternal beauty'. Gino Monaldi perceptively wrote: 'The music of *I Lombardi* can be likened, in a daring simile, to a powerful cascade between rocks and other obstacles; sometimes the stream can be seen breaking forth, sometimes it is hidden; but it never flows evenly and clearly.'

It was appropriate that this opera was dedicated to Duchess Marie Louise of Parma, for her government had investigated and approved Carlo Verdi's application on his son's behalf to the Monte di Pietà, while Marie Louise herself had supported the Milan Conservatory, showing great interest in it. By accepting the dedication, she acknowledged the composer's gratitude as well as recognising the honour he had already brought to the country of his birth.

It is worth recalling perhaps that Verdi, now aged thirty, was still at the beginning of his musical career: by comparison, Schubert was already dead by thirty-one after a life of breath-taking output, which had encompassed operas, masses, piano sonatas, symphonies, chamber music and over six hundred songs.

Marie Louise, Duchess of Parma (1791–1847). She married Napoleon in 1810 and until 1815 was Empress of the French

Chapter 3
Critical Times

'We poor gypsies, charlatans, or whatever you want to call us, are forced to sell our labours, our thoughts and our dreams, for gold'—Verdi

After a flourish in the late eighteenth century when Cimarosa and Paisiello were in their prime, Italian opera had drifted into the doldrums. It was rescued by Gioacchino Rossini. At the age of twenty-one he achieved tremendous success in 1813 with *Tancredi* and *L'Italiana in Algeri*, and then proceeded in ten years to revive and remake Italian opera until he left for Paris in 1823. Six years later, at the age of thirty-seven, he ceased to write operas. He had, however, established a pattern on which his successors, notably Bellini and Donizetti, relied heavily—as one contemporary composer, Pacini, made clear: 'Everyone followed the same school, the same fashions, and as a result they were all imitators of the great luminary. But, good heavens, what else was one to do as there was no other way of making a living? If I was a follower of the great man of Pesaro, so was everyone else.'

Gioacchino Rossini (1792–1868) at about the time of *William Tell*, his last completed opera. Copper engraving by J.C. Thevenin, *circa* 1829–30

With his exuberant orchestral style (including his famous crescendo) and elaborate vocal line, Rossini forged the language of Italian romantic opera, creating forms designed to aid rapid composition. Much of his achievement was to strengthen and refashion what was already there. For example, the dialogue between the set numbers (recitative) had often been accompanied only by the harpsichord, the dry, unadorned sound of which caused it to be known as *recitativo secco*. Various composers had experimented with orchestral accompaniment throughout the opera, but it was Rossini who sounded the death knell of *recitativo secco* in *Elisabetta Regina d'Inghilterra* (*Elizabeth Queen of England*), after which it was rarely used (Verdi's only *recitativo secco* occurs in his disastrous *Un giorno di regno*). This opened the way for a more symphonic treatment of each act or scene as a complete movement, a style Verdi was to explore until in his later operas he provided Italy with his own form of music drama, very different from that fashioned in Germany by his contemporary Wagner.

Felice Varesi (1813–89). Drawing by Kriehuber

Most important in the style of opera construction established by Rossini was the aria in two sections: a slow and expressive air followed by a fast, dazzling section known as the *cabaletta*. Previously composers had merely provided a basic melody leaving the singer great freedom to elaborate and embellish. Rossini, on the other hand, started to write exactly what the singer was to perform, which is why his melodies may seem ornate compared with, for example, those of Mozart or Cimarosa, who expected the singer to provide the ornamentation in accordance with the established practice of the period. A similar formal structure was developed for duets and rondo-finales, but all these set-pieces tended to halt the action, which was carried forward only in the recitatives.

This holding up of the action at those very points where it should be progressing most rapidly was especially evident in the finales at the end of acts. A classic example of this occurs, in fact, in Rossini's own *Il barbiere di Siviglia*, when the soldiers burst into Dr Bartolo's house to find out the cause of the uproar and are greeted by the six principals all offering different explanations at the same time—small wonder that the chorus end the act crying: 'My head seems to be in a fiery smithy, the sound of anvils ceaseless and growing, deafens the ear … thus our poor, bewildered brain, stunned, confounded, in confusion, without reason, is reduced to insanity.' By carrying the dramatic action forward in arias as well as recitative, Verdi was to make each scene or act more an integral unity.

Inheriting a splendidly alive tradition, Verdi imbued all his operas with his own unique style, and yet for many years was partially trapped by the many constraints not only of the Rossinian pattern but also of the accepted customs of the operatic scene. For example, a composer was not free to write parts for whatever voices he chose, since opera houses usually had only a limited number of principal singers. Other parts had therefore to be *comprimario* (or secondary) rôles for singers of lesser ability, but Verdi was generally to extend the number of principals in an opera whilst sharpening the distinction between voice-types, including his particular 'discovery' of the high baritone.

A composer was further constrained by having to write parts specifically suited to individual singers—eighteenth century composers, for instance, often 'tried out' arias on singers and then adapted them as a tailor does a suit after a fitting. Even Verdi was to give Felice Varesi, the baritone, three differently scored versions of the final scene of *Macbeth* so

Gaetano Donizetti
(1797–1848). Drawing by
G. Cammarano

Donizetti insane.
Drawing by Klaus

that he could choose the one he preferred. The *prima donna* reigned supreme, being accustomed to dictate what the composer should write for her, often insisting on finishing an opera with a solo, or even introducing into one opera a favourite aria by another composer. Rossini began to curb this power, and Verdi, following his example, soon expressly forbade alterations.

Restrictions on the text of an opera came not only from the censor but from the librettist himself who, although given pride of place on playbills, was expected to use the texts of popular books and plays rather than write original texts himself. Librettists therefore tended to be conservative and unoriginal in their writing and choice of verse forms. Verdi complained in a letter of 1 January 1853 to Cesare de Sanctis, a Neapolitan friend:

I should like nothing better than to find a good libretto as well as a good poet (we have need of such a one!); but will not conceal from you that I read without pleasure the libretti that are sent to me. It is impossible, or almost impossible, for anyone else to know what it is I want. I want subjects that are new, great, beautiful, varied, strong ... and really strong, with new forms, etc. and at the same time suitable for music.

Another compelling restraint upon opera composers was the Italian public itself which, unlike Parisian audiences, was very conservative, expecting operas to be written 'as they have been before'. Only of his last opera *Falstaff* could Verdi claim: 'I have written it to please myself.' The opera-going public was also insatiable in its demands for more and more operas: Donizetti wrote around seventy-five operas at an average of two a year: between *Nabucco* in 1842 and *Rigoletto* in 1851 Verdi composed twelve operas and completely revised two others, which led him later to refer to these as 'the years of the galley-slave'.

Donizetti failed to add new dimensions to the tradition of Italian romantic opera that owed so much to Rossini. Although he wrote of tragic heroines like Lucia di Lammermoor, Anne Boleyn and Lucrezia Borgia, in these serious operas there is still the same brilliant vocal line, charming melodies, superficial orchestration and swift dramatic movement that characterise his comic opera successes like *Don Pasquale* and *L'elisir d'amore*. Since Donizetti died insane at the age of fifty-one in 1848, it was Verdi who developed the tradition in his own style—'a style transcending the naïvety and pathos of the works of his immediate

Leaving the Grand
Teatro La Fenice in
Venice. Engraving, 1891
(Mary Evans)

predecessors and purged of the more extravagent vulgarities
of grand opera as cultivated in Paris' as Julian Budden has put
it.

Verdi could now afford to be selective in his choice of operas
for, as he declared: 'After *Nabucco* I always had as many
commissions as I wanted.' Presumably, with two major
successes at La Scala, he did not wish to tempt providence
further and so, refusing 'all the kind offers Merelli has made to
me', accepted a contract from Conte Nanni Mocenigo to
produce *I Lombardi* and a new opera, *Ernani*, at Northern Italy's
other major opera house, the Grand Teatro La Fenice in
Venice. Charles Dickens described an evening at the opera in
Venice in *Little Dorrit* published just eleven years after the
première of *Ernani*:

Descending into the sea again after dinner, and ascending out of it
at the Opera staircase, preceded by one of their gondoliers, like an
attendant Merman, with a great linen lantern, they entered their box
… The theatre being dark, and the box light, several visitors lounged
in during the representation … at the close of the performance …
the Merman with his light was ready at the box-door, and other
Mermen with other lights were ready at many of the doors.

Verdi at first thought about setting various works by Byron,
and also considered *King Lear*, an idea to which he was to
return several times during his life. Eventually, however, he

35

Francesco Maria Piave (1810–76), who wrote the libretti of several of Verdi's most famous operas, including *Macbeth*, *Rigoletto*, *La traviata* and *La forza del destino*. Photograph, 1860

agreed to collaborate with Francesco Maria Piave, and together they chose Victor Hugo's *Hernani*, which had been a tremendous success in Paris in 1830. Verdi was faced with a whole variety of problems: the police insisted on minor changes in the libretto; the opera house wanted the part of the bandit chief Ernani made a contralto part for a favourite singer (!); and Mocenigo was shocked at the idea of a horn (which gives the signal for Ernani to take his own life) actually appearing on his historic stage. Just when the composer had won all these battles, the first-night of the Venetian production of *I Lombardi* on 26 December 1843 was a disaster, as Verdi related in a note to Giuseppina Appiani only a quarter of an hour after the fall of the curtain: '*I Lombardi* was a great fiasco: one of the really classic fiascos. Everything was disapproved of, or just tolerated ... that is the simple truth which I relate to you with neither pleasure nor sorrow.'

As the tenor, Domenico Conti, had sung so badly, Verdi had to fight to have him replaced by Carlo Guasco for the forthcoming production of *Ernani*. He had trouble, too, with Sofia Loewe, the soprano, who tried to insist that the final trio be replaced by a solo for her; she even commissioned Piave to write the words, but Verdi, on hearing of this, promptly countermanded the order. The soprano gave in with ill grace, but relations between them, still fairly strained, were made worse by her singing at the *première* on 9 March 1844. Verdi commented: 'Guasco had no voice at all, and was so hoarse it was frightening. It is impossible to sing more out of tune than la Loewe did last night.' Nevertheless this romantic opera, telling the story of the love of three men for one woman, was a success and was soon performed in other European cities, thus giving to its composer a truly international status for the first time. *Ernani* is particularly remarkable for the clear distinction Verdi makes between the tenor, baritone and bass voices, giving to each their own characteristic qualities.

Back in Milan, Verdi started on his next commission—an opera for the Teatro Argentina in Rome. For this he returned to a play by Byron, *The Two Foscari*, that he had previously rejected for performance in Venice. This is hardly surprising since it tells of the repressions and cruelties of the fifteenth century Venetian republic of which a character in Byron's play declares:

.... your midnight carryings off and drownings
Your dungeons next the palace roofs or under
The water's level; your mysterious meetings,
And unknown dooms, and sudden executions
Your 'Bridge of Sighs', your strangling chambers, and
Your torturing instruments have made ye seem
The beings of another and worse world.

The interior of the Grand Teatro La Fenice, the scene of the first performance of *Ernani*

The Basilica of St.
Peter's, Rome.
Engraving (from *Gli
Monumenti più celebri di
Roma antica e moderna*,
Rome 1850)

As was his usual custom, Verdi supervised the writing of the
libretto closely, suggesting many improvements, urging the
long-suffering Piave to 'take a good deal of trouble with it,
because it's a fine subject, delicate and full of pathos'. It is
certainly true that, after the driving force and energy of his
three preceding operas, *I due Foscari* is milder, more
melancholy, with a 'shadowy gloom' conveyed by the delicate
orchestration.

At the end of September Verdi travelled to Rome to
conduct a month of rehearsals, during which, as was his
normal practice, he orchestrated the score. As he approached
'the eternal city' in a carriage for the first time, he must have
shared that magical moment related by so many travellers.
Coming to the crest of a line of hills the coachman would stop
and point into the distance saying: 'Ecco Roma'. ('There is
Rome'). Dr Arnold recounted just such an experience in a
letter to his wife in 1840:

I expected to see St Peter's rising above the line of the horizon, as
York Minster does, but instead of that, it was within the horizon, and
so was much less conspicuous ... but the whole scene that burst upon

our view, when taken in all its parts, was most interesting. Full in front rose the Alban hills, the white villas on their sides distinctly visible, even at that distance, which was more than thirty miles: on the left were the Appennines, and Tivoli was distinctly to be seen on the summit of the chain. On the right, and all before us, lay the Campagna, whose perfectly level outline was succeeded by that of the sea, which was scarcely more so.

I due Foscari was well received at its opening on 3 November, in spite of an audience made hostile by increased seat prices. This short opera is most memorable for Verdi's introduction of themes associated with individual characters, although this is little more than a labelling device nowhere resembling the *leitmotiv* Wagner was to develop. But the future Verdi is evident here, as a critic writing in the *Rivista di Roma* glimpsed: 'Every personage speaks his own language; every character expresses his own passions in a manner evidently dramatic.'

Donizetti wrote to a friend on 26 February 1845 after seeing a performance in Vienna: 'Was I not right to say that Verdi had talent if *I due Foscari* only shows him at his best in fits and starts?' Nevertheless Verdi always had his detractors and none more virulent than the jealous Nicolai who wrote in 1844: 'Look how low Italy has sunk in the last five years. The man

Rome, the Forum. Engraving (*ibid*)

Verdi in 1844, holding a copy of the score of *I due Foscari*

who writes her operas today is Verdi. They are really horrible
.... He scores like a fool—technically he is not even
professional—and he must have the heart of a donkey and in
my view he is a pitiful, despicable composer.'

During this period Verdi took on as his pupil a cobbler's
son, Emanuele Muzio, who, like Verdi himself, had received
the kindly assistance of Barezzi, a grant from the Monte di
Pietà of Busseto, and a refusal of admittance to the Milan
Conservatory. A simple, lovable person, he is chiefly of
interest because of the long letters he wrote to Barezzi, which
have been called 'a monument of ingenuousness, of
mediocrity and devotion', but which nevertheless give
fascinating glimpses of Verdi. Muzio proved invaluable to the
composer for he soon began to act as secretary, answering
letters, turning away the many admiring but unwanted
callers, and dealing with much routine business. He was to
become a trusted friend. In 1846 he declined to compete for
the post of *maestro di musica* of Busseto explaining movingly to
Barezzi:

To tell you the truth I should be extremely sorry to have to
abandon the Signor Maestro after he has given me a second life ... I
don't seem to be his pupil, but rather one of his friends. Always

Emanuele Muzio
(1821–90), later in life.
Oil painting by Boldini

together at lunch, at the coffee house, playing together (for one hour only, from twelve to one); in short he goes nowhere without me accompanying him. At home he has procured a large table and we both write at the same table, and thus I always have the benefit of his advice. It is absolutely impossible for me to abandon him.

Muzio gives a vivid picture of Verdi conducting rehearsals for a revival of *I Lombardi* at La Scala, at this time:

I go to the rehearsals with the Signor Maestro and it makes me sorry to see him tiring himself out; he shouts as if in desperation; he stamps his feet so much that he seems to be playing an organ with pedals, he sweats so much that drops fall on the score … At his glance, at a sign from him, the singers, the chorus and orchestra seem to be touched by an electric spark.

Verdi's next opera, the seventh of his works to be staged, written in a few months, was once more for Merelli and La Scala to a libretto by Solera. Muzio assured their friends in Busseto that *Giovanna D'Arco* (based on Schiller's play) 'will stun all the Milanese' since it contains 'all sorts of music, the theatrical, the religious, the military'. The public in fact did receive it well at the first performance in February 1845 and it was soon performed in other Italian cities, even though the name had to be changed since the censors were suspicious about this female heretic, Joan of Arc (she was not yet canonized), who dies on the battlefield in Verdi's opera and not at the stake. The rôle was created by the soprano Erminia Frezzolini and, although Muzio declared that at rehearsals 'La Frezzolini is always in tears because she says her voice isn't what it used to be', she was a great success. In the streets of Milan the barrel organs and bands were soon playing the catchy demons' chorus.

Merelli immediately asked Verdi to supervise a revival of *Ernani*, but he refused since it had become obvious that La Scala was in a state of decline. Matters were not helped when Verdi discovered that the impresario had been negotiating behind his back with Ricordi for the sale of the full score of *Giovanna D'Arco*. A few months later Merelli staged *I due Foscari* with the second and third acts in the wrong order, so for the next twenty-five years Verdi did not write for the opera house where his career had begun.

Consequently he now agreed to write an opera for the San Carlo Theatre in Naples. Naples was of course a place of great tourist attraction—an essential stop on the 'Grand Tour'—yet

Naples from the West with Vesuvius in the distance. A sketch, *Illustrated London News* (Mary Evans)

Erminia Frezzolini
(1818–84). Drawing by
Kriehuber

it was not a great port, but rather a teeming city, set in a fertile plain, that just happened to be on the coast. The Neapolitan operatic tradition had been immensely strong in the previous century, and correspondingly slow to adapt to Rossini's innovations. At present Mercadante was firmly entrenched there and Pacini's operas much performed. Both thought little of Verdi, though Muzio was later to maintain that the Signor Maestro had caused them 'to gnaw their fingers in jealousy'. Verdi later wrote to Vincenzo Flauto, impresario of the San Carlo, in November 1849, 'to score a real success in Naples is always difficult, particularly for me'.

However he was greatly attracted by being able to work with San Carlo's resident librettist Salvatore Cammarano, whose successes included Donizetti's *Lucia di Lammermoor*. They chose *Alzira*, Voltaire's tale of a Spanish governor of Peru who repents his cruelties on his deathbed, giving his Inca bride to the chief whom she has always loved, thereby converting the Inca to Christianity.

The production had to be postponed for two months owing to the recurrence of an illness that had started to trouble Verdi when composing *I due Foscari*. He complained of bad headaches, stomach pains and a continual sore throat, which seem to have occurred only when he was working on an opera, from which it has been reasonably concluded that they were psychosomatic in origin. Flauto was hard to convince for, as Verdi wryly commented to Cammarano, 'we artists are apparently not allowed to be ill'. The delay was in fact fortunate, since it allowed Eugenia Tadolini, one of Italy's leading sopranos, to recover after the birth of her child, so that she was able to sing in *Alzira* as Verdi wished. Nevertheless, in spite of a fair reception on the first-night on 12 August 1845, it was never very popular, being greeted in almost stony silence in Rome four months later, after which it soon slipped from the repertoire. One contemporary critic sagely remarked in *L'Omnibus*: 'No human talent is capable of producing two or three grand operas a year', and Verdi himself later condemned it roundly: 'Quella è proprio brutta' ('That one is really bad'). There is certainly nothing favourable to Verdi in the comparison of *Alzira* with Wagner's *Tannhaüser*, coincidentally staged that same year, at the Dresden Court Opera.

In a letter to the poet Jacopo Ferretti three months later, Verdi revealed: 'I am very much occupied with *Attila*. What a beautiful subject! The critics may say what they like, but I say "What a beautiful libretto!"' A year earlier Piave had been

Autograph of the last
page of *Attila*, Act I
(British Museum)

given Werner's play *Attila, King of the Huns* to work on, but now Verdi commissioned Solera to produce the libretto for the opera to be given in Venice through the agency of the publisher Francesco Lucca, who was a rival to the house of Ricordi, publishers of *Oberto* and most of Verdi's other operas. Lucca's wife told Verdi: 'When we are in bed, he does nothing but sigh and groan all night': presumably he was thinking of the money he could make if he had the rights to publish one of Verdi's operas. The composer greeted this revelation with ribald amusement; in the end Lucca did succeed in obtaining the publishing rights to *Attila*.

Solera, however, worked incredibly slowly, the exasperated Muzio reporting that he was still in bed at eleven o'clock in the morning. Finally the librettist followed his *prima donna* wife to Barcelona before the last act was completed, so that Piave had to be summoned to complete it. Thus Verdi finally parted from the man with whom he had collaborated on some of his early triumphs. Solera's adventurous life was to continue for he is supposed to have had an affaire with Queen Isabella, edited a religious magazine in Milan, acted as a secret courier for Napoleon III, as spy for Cavour, as a water-carrier in Leghorn and antique dealer in Florence, as well as having been responsible for the suppression of bandits in the Basilicata and the reorganisation of the Egyptian police! He turned up destitute in London in 1875, returning to die in Milan on Easter Sunday 1878.

Verdi's own ill health became worse with the addition of severe gastric trouble, so that he completed *Attila* 'in bed, in an almost dying condition'. Though the opera was produced with 'a fair enough success' on 17 March 1846 at La Fenice, Verdi, in a letter to Contessa Maffei the next day, thought 'the applause and the calls were too much for a poor sick man'. But Italian audiences loved its patriotic flavour, responding to the Roman general's line 'Avrai tu l'universo, resti l'Italia a me' ('You take the universe, but leave Italy to me') with shouts of 'Italy for us!' Muzio wrote to Barezzi on 23 March: '*Attila* has aroused real fanaticism; the Signor Maestro had every imaginable honour: wreaths, and a brass band with torches that accompanied him to his lodgings, amid cheering crowds.'

As his illness grew worse, Verdi was ordered to rest for six months by the doctor, and so he ceased to compose, often driving out into the country or travelling on the new railway from Milan to Monza. The railways had spread rapidly to the Continent after the success of George Stephenson's Liverpool–Manchester railroad opened in 1830, but in Italy progress was slow. The first lines ran only between cities and their suburbs, or between nearby towns. The railways never crossed state boundaries, so that in 1848 the *Annali de Statistica* complained that, although a man could travel at twenty-five miles an hour, it took eight weeks for goods to travel the two hundred kilometres from Florence to Milan. Railways were not the only innovation in Milan for gas lighting had just been introduced there—the world was changing fast.

Verdi, however, still lived very much in the old order of things. Later in the year he went to Recoaro to take the waters, going for long walks and donkey rides in the mountains with Andrea Maffei, recently separated from his wife. Although it would be some years before he was to find freedom from the pressures of the galley-slave years, this period of convalescence, together with the enforced relaxation in the pace of composition, was to lay the foundation for a major step forward in his next opera.

Scene from the first English production of *I Lombardi*; Her Majesty's Theatre, London, 12 May 1846. *Illustrated London News* 23 May 1846 (Mary Evans)

Chapter 4
'The Years Of The Galley Slave'

'What sublime music! I can tell you there are things that make one's hair stand on end!'—Muzio (on *Macbeth*)

As the six months of convalescence ordered by the doctor drew towards the autumn of 1846 the demands of the operatic world began to force themselves once more on Verdi, for as usual the impresarios had been convinced only with difficulty by the medical certificates declaring that he could not 'write music without grave risk to his health and perhaps even to his life'. Flauto of Naples, having previous experience of the composer's illness, released him from his contract; Léon Escudier agreed to postpone an opera which Verdi had agreed to direct in Paris; Benjamin Lumley, the English impresario, had also, rather unwillingly, agreed to wait; Lucca, ever mindful of gain, was still pressing for two more operas. Verdi however arranged to write one for Lanari to be given at the Teatro della Pergola in Florence and published not by Lucca, who had had the temerity to argue over the choice of subject, but once more by Ricordi.

After considering various subjects, Verdi settled on Shakespeare's *Macbeth* and produced a synopsis himself which he sent in September 1846 to Piave with the admonition: 'This tragedy is one of the greatest creations of man ... If we can't make something great out of it let us at least try to do something out of the ordinary.'

Poor Piave was bullied mercilessly by the composer who found faults, suggested amendments, dictated the verse metres, yet even then was not satisfied with the finished libretto as he made abundantly clear in a letter of 21 January 1847: 'Of course you're not the slightest bit in the wrong except for having neglected those last two acts in an incredible way. Well, it can't be helped; Sant' Andrea [Count Maffei] has come to my rescue and yours—and more especially to mine,

since to be frank I couldn't have set your verses to music. Still
we've managed to put it all right now—by changing almost
everything, however.' Certainly Maffei completely rewrote the
witches' chorus in Act III and Lady Macbeth's sleepwalking
scene. Piave's name was omitted from the title page, although
Verdi paid him in full. Fortunately, Piave did not take
umbrage or refuse to write again for Verdi to his eternal
credit, for their future collaboration was to produce, amongst
others, Verdi's best-loved opera—*La traviata*.

The Maestro must have been almost unbearable in his
concern that everything should be right for the production of
Macbeth, making quite clear to Lanari, for example, how many
witches there should be, suggesting that the new 'magic
lantern' should be used for the apparitions, and giving strict
instructions that Banquo's ghost 'must come from under the
earth' through a trapdoor. 'All these ideas I've got from
London where they've been playing *Macbeth* continuously over
the last two hundred years', he wrote on 22 December 1846.
Verdi certainly had a great affinity with Shakespeare. In a
letter to Escudier he was emphatic in his rejection of criticism
of the later Paris production:

Oh, there they are greatly mistaken. It may be that I did not do
Macbeth justice, but to say I do not know, I do not understand and do
not feel Shakespeare, no, by God, no! He is my favourite poet. I have
known him from my childhood and read and reread him carefully.

Arriving in Florence a month before the *première*, he found
that Sofia Loewe, whose voice had suddenly gone, had been

Marianna Barbiere-Nini (1820–87) who created the rôle of Lady Macbeth. Copper engraving by M. Menghini, 1844

replaced by Marianna Barbiere-Nini in the part of Lady Macbeth. She later recalled that Verdi rehearsed her duet in the first act with Felice Varesi, the baritone, as Macbeth,

more than one hundred and fifty times, so that it might be, as Verdi used to say, more *spoken than sung*. And imagine this. The evening of the final rehearsal, with a theatre full of guests, Verdi made the artists put on their costumes, and when he insisted on something woe to anyone contradicting him. [Dress rehearsals were almost unheard of at that time.] When we were dressed and ready, the orchestra in the pit, the chorus on stage, Verdi signalled to me and Varesi to follow him into the wings. There he explained that he wanted us to accompany him to the foyer for another piano rehearsal of that accursed duet.

'Maestro', I protested. 'We are already in our Scottish costumes; how can we?'

'Put a cloak over them.'

And Varesi, annoyed at the strange request, dared to raise his voice: 'But we've already rehearsed it a hundred and fifty times, for God's sake!'

'I wouldn't say that again, for within half an hour it will be a hundred and fifty-one!'

He was tyrant who had to be obeyed. I can still remember the black look Varesi shot at Verdi as he followed the Maestro into the foyer. With his hand clutching the pommel of his sword he seemed about to murder Verdi even as later he would murder King Duncan. But even Varesi gave in, and the hundred-and-fifty-first rehearsal

Verdi in 1847. Copper engraving by Geoffroy

took place, while the impatient audience made an uproar in the theatre. But anyone who said merely that the duet was enthusiastically received would be saying nothing at all; for it was something incredible, new, unimagined ...

The *première* on 14 March 1847 was a sensation with Verdi taking at least twenty-five curtain calls, and being escorted home by cheering crowds, after he had been to thank his leading lady:

The storm of applause had not yet died down, and I was standing in my dressing-room, trembling and exhausted, when the door flew open—I was already half undressed—and Verdi stood before me. He gesticulated and his lips moved as if he wanted to speak but could not utter a word. Between tears and laughter, I too could say nothing. But I saw his eyes were red. He squeezed my hand very tightly and rushed out. That moment of real feeling paid me many times over for the months of hard work and continuous agitation.

He dedicated *Macbeth*, undoubtedly his greatest opera to date, to his old friend and patron Barezzi. Apologising that he had not previously dedicated an opera to his benefactor, he wrote in a letter of 25 March 1847:

Here is this *Macbeth* which I love more than all my other operas and which I think the most worthy present to you. It comes from my heart: let yours receive it, and let it always be a witness of the gratitude and affection borne for you by

Your most affectionate
G. VERDI.

Eighteen years later he was to revise it almost completely for a Paris production at the suggestion of his French publisher, Léon Escudier, and it is this 1865 version that is usually performed today, although it was not particularly successful when first produced.

Verdi's *Macbeth* of 1847 was published in Italy at the same time as Charlotte Brontë's *Jane Eyre* and her sister Emily's *Wuthering Heights* were published in England. The event of the year that Verdi himself is most likely to have heard of, however, was the death in November of Mendelssohn, shortly after yet another triumphant visit to England, a country that was not to forget his memory throughout the reign of Victoria.

While in Florence, Verdi went on many tours of the ancient city—'the Athens of the north'—meeting the Grand Duke, and impressing men like the poet Giuseppe Giusti, and the sculptor Dupré, of whom he became a lifelong friend, with his knowledge of, and interest in, painting and sculpture, particularly the works of Michaelangelo. Also in Florence was

Andrea Maffei, already at work on an operatic version of Schiller's *Die Räuber* (*The Brigands*), which was to become the text for Verdi's next opera.

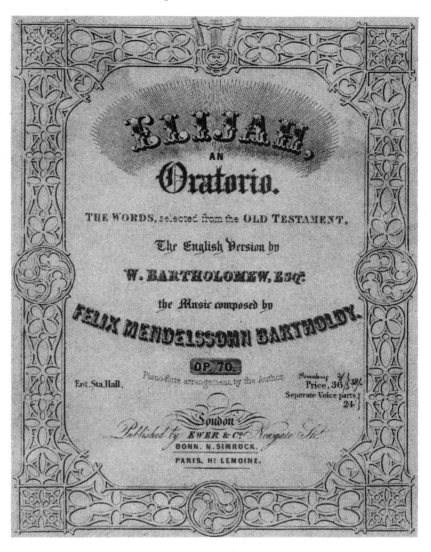

The title page of the original English vocal score of Mendelssohn's *Elijah,* first performed at the Birmingham Festival, 26 August 1846 (Ateş Orga)

I masnadieri, as it came to be called, was to be given at Her Majesty's Theatre, London, for the English impresario Benjamin Lumley and the Italian publisher Lucca. Verdi, accompanied by the faithful Muzio, set out in May 1847 travelling by way of Switzerland and Strasbourg, then down the Rhine by steamer to Cologne, finally reaching Paris by way of Brussels. Muzio was sent on alone to London to make advance arrangements. When Verdi arrived there a few days later, his reactions to England's capital city were mixed, as he

London street scene
(Mary Evans)

made clear in a letter to Giuseppina Appiani written on 27 June 1847:

> Long live our sun, which I have always loved greatly, but which I now adore, since I've been suffering this fog and smoke which suffocates me and depresses me as well. Apart from that, what a magnificent city! There are things here at which you stare as though turned to stone—but this climate paralyses such beauty. Oh, if only the Naples sky were here, you wouldn't need to ask for Paradise.

Muzio, too, recorded his impressions of London in a long and amusing letter earlier in the same month to Barezzi:

> What a chaos is London! What confusion! ... People shouting, poor people weeping, steamers flying, men on horseback, in carriages, on foot, and all howling like the damned. My dear Signor Antonio, you can't imagine what it's like.

Their reactions are not surprising for the new railroad tracks, tunnels, viaducts, bridges, steam and smoke had altered the landscape drastically, bringing more people into the capital. The lumbering coaches of the past and the famous coaching inns were fast giving way to the railway, with the main London *termini* and their station hotels. Wordsworth, who died in 1850, was simply one among many voices raised against 'the monstrous ant-hill' whose grim face of dirt,

Railway construction at Blackfriars, London, looking towards Ludgate Hill and St Paul's Cathedral.
Illustrated London News (Mary Evans)

despair, overcrowding, appalling conditions, poverty and vice was captured in Charles Dickens' novels written at this time.

Because of the fog and the smoke, Verdi stayed in a great deal, getting up at five in the morning and working until six at night, then going to the theatre where Lumley had placed a box at his disposal. Muzio 'stared his eyes out' at the rich dresses, diamonds and jewellery; the ladies in their turn, as a newspaper recorded, 'devoured poor Verdi with their opera-glasses'. He refused nearly all the social invitations that poured in, including one from Queen Victoria, but that august lady made the *première* of *I masnadieri* a Command Performance on 22 July, attending with Prince Albert, other members of the Royal Family, and Parliament. Muzio recorded:

The opera aroused a furore. From the prelude to the last finale there was nothing but applause, *evvivas*, recalls and encores. The Maestro himself conducted, seated on a chair higher than all the others, baton in hand ... The Maestro was cheered, called on the stage, alone and with the singers, flowers were thrown to him, and nothing was heard but '*Viva Verdi, bietifol*' [beautiful].

Jenny Lind, 'the Swedish Nightingale', acted admirably, and sang the airs allotted to her exquisitely, but Luigi Lablache, who had made such an excellent and corpulent Dr Dulcamara in Donizetti's *L'elisir d'amore*, was ill-suited to portray an old man 'reduced to a skeleton' by long imprisonment. Verdi felt that the opera had been 'well received'. Lumley wrote later in his memoirs that, although the first-night had the appearance of a triumph, *I masnadieri* 'could not be considered a success … [and] was never successful on an Italian stage'. However, he did want Verdi to stay on as musical director of Her Majesty's, but the composer, no doubt considering that only a high reward could reconcile him to the English climate, asked such an exorbitant fee that the matter was dropped and Verdi returned to Paris.

Paris was in a restless state at this time. After the excesses of the 1789 Revolution and the rise and fall of Napoleon, the restoration of the monarchy under Louis XVIII and Charles X had not been successful. The Revolution of 1830 took place almost entirely in Paris and instituted the bourgeois monarchy of Louis Philippe 'the citizen king'. His reign of eighteen years was coming to an end as Verdi arrived in Paris. The popular heir to the throne, the Duke of Orleans, had been killed in a carriage accident in 1842; there was a growing sense of disenchantment with King Louis Philippe and resentment at the lack of any liberal measures. The republican uprising of 24 February 1848 that was to bring the barricades onto the streets of Paris once more was just around the corner. The old and tired King was to abdicate, retiring to a villa in Surrey, leaving the way open for the return of Napoleonic rule under the Emperor's nephew, Louis Bonaparte.

The golden years of the Paris Opéra were the 1830s and 40s.

A scene from the first performance of *I masnadieri*, Her Majesty's Theatre, London, 22 July 1847, with Jenny Lind (1820–87) and Luigi Lablache (1794–1858). The *Illustrated London News* wrote: 'The great object of attraction is still Verdi's new opera, possessing, as it does, so much additional interest from the fact of its being one of the first operas ever written for our Anglo-Italian stage. We hope, however, it will not be the last and that, the example once set, will be frequently followed. It redounds greatly to the credit of the management that this important step in art should have been taken in a season which all prophesied would be one of extraordinary difficulties for Her Majesty's Theatre, and which, on the contrary, will have been one of the most brilliant in its annals' (Mary Evans)

Louis Philippe, 'The Citizen King' (1773–1850). Etching by A. Hervieu, 1835 (from Frances Trollope's *Paris and the Parisians*, Vol. II, London 1836)

The Opéra had always drawn Italian composers across the Alps, and now Verdi followed Cherubini, Rossini and Donizetti among others by agreeing to Léon Escudier's suggestion that he should produce a completely revised version of *I Lombardi* in French for the Opéra in collaboration with the poets Alphonse Royer and Gustave Vaëz. The *première* of *Jérusalem* on 26 November 1847 went well enough for Louis Philippe to have two acts performed before him at the Tuileries, for which he created Verdi a Chevalier de la Légion d'Honneur. Ricordi published the Italian score with a dedication to the now retired singer, Giuseppina Strepponi, who had been such a help to Verdi in his early career and who now began to figure more prominently in his life.

Undoubtedly the composer had seen his former *prima donna* on his way to London during his brief stop in Paris, where she had been living and teaching for over a year, but on his return they must have met a great deal. Opinion has differed considerably as to when they became lovers but, while there is no evidence to support the view that they were lovers as early as 1842, we do know that their friendship developed considerably during 1847.

Ursula Günther, a German Verdi scholar, has recently discovered in a manuscript of *Jérusalem* the words of the love-duet filled in alternately in Verdi's and Strepponi's handwriting, indicating a secret and early declaration of their love. Undoubtedly something had happened to keep the composer in Paris for two years, when he had originally intended to stay for only a few weeks. Although he offered various excuses—his contract with the Opéra, negotiations for a further contract, and finally his illness—there is now little doubt that the real reason was Giuseppina Strepponi.

She was the daughter of a musician, who died at the age of thirty-four having written a few operas. She had gone, like

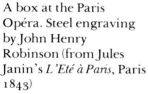

A box at the Paris Opéra. Steel engraving by John Henry Robinson (from Jules Janin's *L'Eté à Paris*, Paris 1843)

Strepponi in 1845. Oil painting, anonymous

The publisher Francesco Lucca (1802–72). Lithograph by Doyen

Verdi, to the Milan Conservatory winning the first prize there for *bel canto*, launching in 1834 on an immensely successful operatic career. She was soon recognised as a *prima donna assoluta*, yet her private life had its very considerable problems that certainly caused a great deal of speculation. She gave birth to an illegitimate son, Camillino, in 1837, and a second child about four years later, having had a miscarriage in the meantime. At the time many, including Verdi, believed her to be the mistress of Merelli, the Milan impresario, but modern research (by Frank Walker) has shown that the father of both her children was the tenor, Napoleone Moriani.

Not only had things gone wrong with her private life, but she had greatly overtaxed her voice, sometimes giving as many as five, or even seven, performances a week. The strain showed itself in fits of coughing which the doctors threatened would lead to consumption unless she gave up singing altogether. *Nabucco* was almost the end of her career. Solera paid her a lasting tribute when he admired in her:

the most beautiful natural gifts rendered great by continual study, so that in both the serious style and the comic she caused the many celebrated singers who had preceded her to be forgotten. Gifted with extreme sensitivity, she knows how to win the hearts of the spectators by her voice and her expression ... Who is there that did not weep at her tears ... in *Lucia* ... and who is there who was not made happy by her laugh in that delightful jest by Romani and Donizetti *L'elisir d'amore*? ... Deny if you can that singers are rare indeed whom both serious and comic roles suit so well.

Giuseppina greatly resented the fact that Verdi, her lover, was forced to continue his work under pressure from impresarios and publishers, particularly Francesco Lucca, with whom he was still under contract to produce another opera. Their correspondence was full of ill-concealed hostility on the composer's part, as he resisted Lucca's suggestions of another librettist instead of Piave, as well as for alternative subjects to Byron's *The Corsair* (a tale of Greek pirates fighting the Turks) upon which Piave had already begun work. 'I may be making a big mistake', wrote Verdi flatly, 'but it is *The Corsair* or nothing. All your arguments against it only make me like the subject more.' In fact he seems to have started the project with a considerable enthusiasm that waned later.

His annoyance with the 'most irritating and ungrateful' Lucca who 'forced me to finish *Attila* in a deplorable physical condition' meant that he did not take a great deal of trouble over *Il corsaro*. He completed it in a few months, and sent it off to the impresario telling him laconically to make whatever use

Fighting in the streets of
Milan, 22 March 1848
(Mary Evans)

of it he thought best. In fact Lucca put it on (after a
postponement caused by the *Cinque Giornate*, the Five Day
Revolt) at the Teatro Grande in Trieste on 25 October 1848.
Verdi was not at the *première* as he 'didn't feel fit to undertake
the long and tiring journey at this time of year'. It was just as
well, for the *première* was a disaster with only the scene designer
receiving a curtain call and the opera vanished from the
repertoire after three performances. Nevertheless, in spite of
the fact that Verdi later dismissed it as 'dull and ineffective'
and others have said it is 'best forgotten', it does have
moments, especially the prison scene, that rise above the
ordinary to stir the emotions and quicken the responses.

1848 was demonstrably a year more memorable for other
things: the discovery of gold in California, the publication of
Marx and Engels' *Communist Manifesto*, the first Public Health
Act in Britain, the appearance of Thackeray's *Vanity Fair*, the
deaths of Donizetti and of Emily Brontë. It was also, of course,
the year of revolutions when all Europe was in turmoil.

After the toppling of Louis Philippe in France by the
workers' revolt, the students in Vienna, for instance, followed
suit forcing Metternich, for forty years the bastion of Austrian
repressive politics, to join the French King in exile in England.
Immediately, while the Venetians under the lawyer Daniele
Manin declared a republic in an almost bloodless coup, the
Milanese attacked the Governor's palace and in the next few
days put up nearly 1,700 barricades in the streets, defending

them against the Austrian troops with bottles, tiles, paving stones and an odd assortment of arms. This glorious *Cinque Giornate* revolt ended after King Carlo Alberto of Piedmont had intervened, forcing the Austrian army under Radetzky to withdraw from Milan.

Hearing the news, Verdi rushed to Milan, arriving in early April no doubt hoping to be part of that movement by which, in Carlo Alberto's words: 'L'Italia fara da se' ('Italy will act on its own'). Verdi wrote to Piave on 21 April 1848: 'I am drunk with joy. Just think: there are no more Germans here!!' and in another letter: 'I've been unable to see anything except those marvellous barricades. All honour to our brave champions. Honour to all Italy who at this moment is really great. You may be sure that the hour of her freedom has struck. The people will have it so.'

However, after the first flush of victory there was considerable political disorder. This confusion was caused in part by the slow communications of the times. (Although the telegraph had been invented in 1848, it was still not in general use, so horseback courier and mailcoach were the fastest ways for news to travel. Rowland Hill had introduced the Penny Post in England in 1840, but letters on the Continent were very slow—Milan to Paris, five days; Venice to London, twelve.) Carlo Alberto and the Piedmontese naturally wanted Milan and Lombardy to be annexed to them, but the city leaders, including Manzoni, refused. Yet they hesitated to follow Venice by declaring a republic, much to the fury of republicans like Mazzini and Verdi, who wrote again to Piave: 'Banish every petty municipal idea! We must all extend a fraternal hand, and Italy will yet become the first nation of the world.' Any hope of achieving a quick, concerted victory vanished when Pope Pius IX published his Allocution on the 29 April in which he refused to countenance the fight against the Austrians. By the end of May, when it had become clear that the republican cause was lost, Verdi returned to Paris; but not before he had bought, in exchange for a small farm at Le Roncole where he had previously settled his parents, a farm at Sant' Agata near Busseto that was to become his home and which remains in the Verdi family to this day.

Back in Paris the Revolution had thrown everything into confusion: business and industry were at a standstill, and the unemployed had turned the Champs Elysées into a kind of fair-ground with jugglers, acrobats, fortune-tellers, patent medicine sellers and the like entertaining the mob who were becoming more and more disillusioned with the Republic.

Verdi rejoined Giuseppina in Paris in time to witness the fearful events of June when the 'Red Republicans' turned on the Moderates and slaughtered many at the barricades. *The Illustrated London News* recorded on 1 July 1848: 'Among the many fearful episodes of the struggle, it is related that the heads of many of them were cut off by women and stuck on poles at the head of a barricade which they had lost their lives in attempting to storm.'

The Archbishop of Paris, attempting to reason with the insurgents in the Place de la Bastille, was shot in the loins from behind and died after twenty-four hours of great agony. General Cavaignac was given power to put down the rebellion by the National Assembly, which he did with extreme savagery. However, Verdi was one of the signatories of an appeal to him for French military aid for Carlo Alberto after his defeat at the Battle of Custoza. As the appeal was ignored, Carlo Alberto signed the armistice of Salasco with Radetzky. The refugees streamed out of Milan, including the Contessa Maffei who fled to Switzerland, and Mazzini who went to Lugano. In October 1848 Verdi sent him a patriotic hymn *Suona la tromba* (*Sound the trumpet*) to words by the poet Mameli, which Mazzini hoped would become the Italian *Marseillaise*, while Verdi expressed the wish that it would 'soon be sung on the plains of Lombardy, amid the music of the cannon'. Unfortunately neither of these hopes was fulfilled since Verdi, the composer who most signified Italian aspirations, was not really suited to the writing of a national anthem for the country he loved so dearly.

However his thoughts now turned towards a specifically nationalistic opera in collaboration with Cammarano, after a change of management at the San Carlo had enabled him to dispense with a contract committing him to write another work for Naples. Cammarano based his libretto on Joseph Méry's *La bataille de Toulouse*—the story of the Lombard League's defeat of the Holy Roman Emperor and German King, Frederick Barbarossa, in 1176, which would certainly never have been permitted by the strict Neopolitan censorship. So the *première* of *La battaglia di Legnano* (*The Battle of Legnano*) took place in the Teatro Argentina at Rome during the carnival season on 27 January 1849 a fortnight before Rome was declared a republic by the newly-elected Assembly, Pio Nono having fled to the Kingdom of the Two Sicilies after the murder of Rossi, his chief administrator. With a finale built round the line 'Chi muore par la patria alma si rea non ha' ('He who dies for his country does not have a guilty soul'),

Title page of the original vocal score of *La battaglia di Legnano*

it naturally created a 'furore', the audience at every performance wearing republican cockades, waving banners, throwing streamers and singing lustily with the chorus. When the hero leapt from a balcony into a moat in order to join the fight, one account has it that a soldier in the audience was so overcome that he jumped from the gallery into the orchestra pit. One contemporary critic declared: 'Far from following the old conventions, Verdi has felt that his spirit needs freedom just as Italy needs independence.' Yet *La battaglia di Legnano* never escaped the stigma of being a *pièce d'occasion* and, although the composer thought well of it, it fell foul of the censors even though it was presented in several other guises.

Verdi had gone to Rome for the opening but returned thereafter to Paris and Giuseppina, hoping to return soon to Italy as he assured Piave, who was now acting as a 'citizen-soldier' in besieged Venice. Italian military fortunes now began to slump: Carlo Alberto renounced the armistice but was defeated by Radetzky at the Battle of Novara and forced to abdicate; the Roman republic was overturned and the Pope reinstalled by French troops; and Garibaldi made his epic retreat towards Venice, which itself collapsed after a siege. Republican hopes were for the moment dashed, but, as Manin declared to the Venetians on quitting the city: 'We have sown the good seed; it will fructify in good soil.'

Perhaps disgusted by the French intervention at Rome, and probably wishing to avoid the cholera outbreak in Paris, Verdi

61

The Teatro Argentina in Rome, where the *première* of *La battaglia di Legnano* was staged. A photograph

returned to Busseto, where he completed his next opera *Luisa Miller* at the Palazzo Orlandi, while Giuseppina settled the eleven-year old Camillino in Florence. 'Farewell my joy' she wrote to Verdi in September 1849, 'I should like to be able to fly to your side'. Her eventual arrival at Busseto scandalized the local people, providing the subject of gossip for many years to come, during which she was to suffer much from the small town inhabitants' cruel words and social ostracism. She and her lover kept very much to themselves, reflecting his inflexible attitude to public opinion which he made plain to Flauto, the Neapolitan impresario:

I must confess I am more of a bear than before. I have been working constantly now for six years, and wandering from country to country, and I have never said a word to a journalist, never begged a friend, never courted rich people to achieve success. Never, absolutely never! I shall always despise such methods. I write my operas as well as I can: for the rest, I let things take their course without ever influencing public opinion to the slightest degree.

In the end Verdi had been forced to honour his contract with the San Carlo if only to safeguard Cammarano, who was being threatened by the management with imprisonment for failure to supply the libretto based on Schiller's play *Kabale und Liebe,* a tale, as the title says, of intrigue and love. *Luisa Miller* has rightly been called a transitional work. The first two acts contain the set pieces linked by recitative belonging to the world of Bellini and Donizetti, while the third act has much more sense of continuity and also a quality of tenderness and intimacy that is new in Verdi's music.

Completing work on it by the end of October, (the month, incidentally, of Chopin's death) Verdi set out for Naples with Barezzi, taking his former father-in-law sight-seeing to the islands, including Capri, and the mainland tourist attractions of Pompeii, Vesuvius and Herculaneum. Samuel Rogers in his *Italian Journal 1814–1821* conveyed vividly the impression made on him by visits to the same places:

Went to Pompeii, winding along the shore and round Vesuvius. We had no intimation of what was coming—when, alighting at a small door, we descended a few paces, and found ourselves in the forum, the columns of the portico standing, and on some of them scrawled by the people names, a horse galloping in red chalk—then came the theatres, the basilica, the temples, the streets—after passing the Apothecary's, who can stand at the fountain—where the three ways meet paved with lava—and look up and down near the oil-merchant's door and the miller's, and not feel a strange and not unpleasant sadness? ... The ruins round the base of Vesuvius may be compared to the bones that strew the ground at the mouth of a Lion's den; who is only sleeping within—and growling in his slumber—the lava-streets, the wheel-tracks, the stepping-stones, the

Title page of the original vocal score of *Luisa Miller*

names and figures scrawled on the columns in the forum, the worn steps, the stone-seats by the way-side, the iron hooks in the door posts for the hinges to move on, the stone-counters and earthern jars in the oil-merchant's shop, the circular stains of the cups on the marble slab in the liquor shop.

The intrepid tourist also went up Vesuvius on a pony, noting as he went the lizards sunning themselves on stones and a 'cicada flying across the road like a little bird'. The last part of the ascent was made on foot until they stood on the brink of the 'black and sulphurous crater':

The noise was not continual, but by fits—The silence that came continually rendering it still more awful—a noise now deep and hollow, like the rolling and dashing of waters—now sharp and clattering like that of a Forge such as Virgil [who composed the *Georgics* in Naples] places in Etna—and now like the explosion of great Ordnance or of thunder among mountains—the noise instantly followed by a discharge of large substances, most of them red hot, many of which fall back into the abyss, and many against the sides with a violent crash—and some at our feet and behind us. In the air they appeared like shells thrown by an enemy, and the danger was not small, my two guides continually pulling me by the arm, and crying 'Andiamo, Signor' ['Come on, Sir']—Those that fell near us were lighted cinders near a foot square, and red as when dropping or

The Ruins of Pompeii, 1855 (Mary Evans)

The Teatro San Carlo in Naples

shot out from a fire ... Stood awhile on the brow of the mountain, now looking down on Herculaneum and Pompeii and Stabia and now on the horrid gulf. It was an awful and interesting thing to connect them in one's mind, the Sun shining on the sea and the shore—all so lovely and smiling so near the mouth that may devour them all.

Squabbles with the management of the theatre over payment led to the ridiculous sight of Verdi threatening to board a French warship in the bay with his opera to protect himself from being kept forcibly in Naples. On the first-night on 8 December 1849 *Luisa Miller* was a fair success, although some scenery collapsed narrowly missing the composer, a mishap attributed by his friends to the presence of one Capecelatro who was said to have the 'Evil Eye' and at whose doorstep the failure of *Alzira* in Naples four years earlier had been laid.

Consequently he decided to write the next opera with Cammarano for Ricordi. They decided not to tackle the Shakespearian plays *King Lear*, *The Tempest* and *Hamlet* because 'these huge subjects demand too much time ... and, pushed as I am by two commissions, I have had to choose easier and shorter subjects to be able to fulfil my obligations'.

So, while Liszt was producing Wagner's *Lohengrin* at Weimar, Verdi and Piave, instead of Cammarano, combined to produce in rapid time *Stiffelio*, based on a French play about a protestant minister whose wife, having committed adultery,

65

Trieste, where the *premières* of *Il corsaro* and *Stiffelio* were given at the Teatro Grande. Engraving by A.H. Payne (Mary Evans)

wants a divorce, but is finally forgiven by her husband. Such a story was obviously difficult for Italian audiences unused to clerical marriage, let alone divorce, and to whom the idea of a wronged husband not taking revenge was almost unthinkable. The libretto ran into considerable trouble with the censor when Ricordi decided to hold the *première* in Trieste, but major changes saved it from being banned altogether and it was given first on 16 November 1850.

There are signs in this opera, as in its predecessor, that Verdi was moving into a new stage of creative writing. The 'galley-slave years' were coming to an end, and, as the nineteenth century passed into its second half, Verdi's next opera was to mark a turning point in his own career, in the history of Italian opera and indeed in the development of music.

Chapter 5
Tragic Triumphs

'He wept and loved for us all'—D'Annunzio

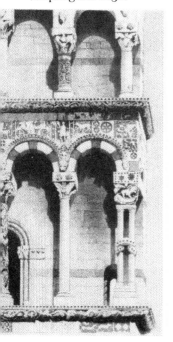

An illustration of ornate Venetian wall-veil decoration, San Michele, Lucca, from John Ruskin's *The Stones of Venice*, Vol. II (Orpington 1851)

As it is built on a group of islands, Venice has a unique character and beauty. For centuries it had been an important trading centre, so the Most Serene Republic had become extremely wealthy—a wealth used to create a city of magnificent buildings containing some of Europe's finest art treasures. Change had come however. The first bridge linking Venice with the mainland had been opened in 1846. This carried the Venice-Vicenza railway that not only provided a stimulus to the Venetian economy but also profoundly affected the way of life of a city that had hitherto relied solely on water-borne transportation. A large section of the bridge had to be deliberately destroyed when the Austrians besieged Manin's Venetian Republic. In spite of the cannon bombardment that eventually caused Manin to capitulate in August 1849, Venice still preserved much of her precious beauty and splendour as travellers of the time were to be shown by the publication in 1851 and 1853 of the three volumes of John Ruskin's *The Stones of Venice*.

Verdi's next opera *Rigoletto*, was to be for the Teatro La Fenice there. With Piave he chose Victor Hugo's play *Le Roi s'amuse* before *Stiffelio* was even produced. He wrote an enthusiastic letter to the librettist in May 1850:

Le Roi s'amuse is the greatest subject and perhaps the greatest drama of modern times. Triboulet is a creation worthy of Shakespeare!! ... going over the various subjects in my mind *Le Roi* came on me like a flash of lightning, an inspiration, and I said to myself ... 'Yes, by God, that one can't go wrong!'

Because it depicted King François I as a debauched libertine which, in those revolutionary days, was an image of royalty that could not be countenanced by the authorities (however true it really was), the play had caused a great scandal when

The Austrian
bombardment of
Venice, 1849 (Mary
Evans)

first given at the Théâtre Français, Paris in 1832, so that no
further performances took place in France for fifty years.

In anticipation of censorship difficulties in Italy, Verdi
instructed Piave to 'run about the city and find someone of
influence' to sanction it. Having received his assurances that
all was well, Verdi started to sketch out the work in his mind.
The libretto was finished by October, but early in December
Verdi was stunned to receive from Marzari, President of La
Fenice, an official letter stating categorically that:

His Excellency the Military Governor Chevalier de Gorzkowski in
his respected dispatch of the 26th instant directs me to communicate
to you his profound regret that the poet Piave and the celebrated
Maestro Verdi have not chosen some other field to display their
talents than the revolting immorality and obscene triviality forming
the story of the libretto *La Maledizione* (*The Curse*), submitted to us for
eventual performance at La Fenice.

His Excellency has decided that the performance must be absolutely forbidden and wishes me at the same time to request you not to make further inquiries in this matter.

Luckily everything was not quite so final, for discussions with the censor's office continued for a month until the major cause of offence—the portrayal of the depravity of a reigning monarch—was removed by changing the setting to Mantua and renaming all the characters. Thus Hugo's Triboulet became Rigoletto (from the French *rigoler*, to laugh). Amongst the censor's objections was the fact that the jester was a hunchback, but Verdi defended this in a letter of 14 December 1850:

A Hunchback who sings? Why not? ... I thought it would be beautiful to portray this extremely deformed and ridiculous character who is inwardly passionate and full of love. I chose the subject precisely because of these qualities and these original traits, and if they are cut I shall no longer be able to set it to music.

Some alterations were made, however, to tone down the licentiousness of the Duke, although Verdi insisted that he must be shown as a libertine who is cursed for seducing the daughter of one of his subjects, for 'without this curse, what scope or significance does the drama have?'

Verdi and Piave made the curse central to the drama, intending originally to call the opera *La maledizione*. The curse is laid on the Duke and his jester, Rigoletto, the encourager of his master's excesses, by the aged Count Monterone whose

Title page of the original vocal score of *Rigoletto*

Rigoletto, autograph
sketch for Rigoletto's
aria, Act II (G. Ricordi &
Co.)

daughter the Duke has seduced. The curse is worked out as Rigoletto's daughter. Gilda, the sole joy in his dark life, is herself seduced by the very man the jester has encouraged. But the curse reaches further still, for, when Rigoletto plans the Duke's death, it is his daughter who dies, and the opera ends as the hunchback, finding his daughter's body in a sack, despairingly cries: 'Ah! La maledizione!' The dark horror of the opera is heightened by moments of tender emotion—Rigoletto's gentle love of Gilda, and her aria 'Caro nome' ('Beloved name') in which she sings of her love for the Duke.

But it is in the third act that Verdi, without consciously innovating, leaves previous operatic convention behind and, by making the scene rather than the aria the important unit, creates a musical structure that must surely rate as one of the finest he wrote. With its rich use of orchestral motifs, with duets and arias arising out of the recitative so that their beginning and end cannot easily be distinguished, and above all with the marvellously sustained creation of atmosphere in the squalor of the inn and the violence of the storm, the act nevertheless does not lose the vivid portrayal of each individual character that is such a step forward in Verdi's mastery. For example, the jaunty and inconsequential (though utterly memorable) tune of the Duke's well-known 'La donna è mobile' only serves to highlight his shallow yet ruthless nature; while, in the famous quartet that follows, each character clearly retains his or her own identity and emotions within a tightly constructed ensemble.

Approval for *Rigoletto* was given only four weeks before the scheduled *première* on 11 March 1851. This was a triumphant success, although the reviewers seemed unable to agree about the novelty of the piece. Yet it has always firmly retained its place in the regular operatic repertoire, as a striking landmark in the history of opera and, as Verdi himself remarked, 'the best subject as regards theatrical effect that I've ever set to music. It has powerful situations, variety, excitement, pathos.' On hearing it Rossini exclaimed: 'In this music I at last recognize Verdi's genius.'

Shortly after this, having previously settled his parents at a house in nearby Vidalenzo, Verdi moved with Giuseppina to 'our country house', the farmhouse at Sant' Agata. They lived a very secluded life, having practically nothing to do with Busseto and very little with the rest of the world. They both consulted together about the planning of the garden round the house, although Giuseppina later noted ruefully that what had started out as her garden soon became 'my garden' to

The villa at Sant' Agata.
A photograph

Verdi as his interest in country matters quickened. They planted trees and shrubs and laid out a very attractive garden through which they could walk to the fields. Verdi supervised the work of his three tenant farms, keeping scrupulous accounts of wine, corn, hay, manure, flour, salt and the livestock transactions. Eighteen months after they had moved to Sant' Agata there were four oxen, seventeen cows, ten bullocks, eleven calves and six rams.

Although Verdi had supported his parents, there was some friction between father and son, so that in January 1851 the composer had to write to Dr Ercolano Balestra, a notary in Busseto, making it clear that his father was not in charge of the administration of the estate. 'I intend to be quite separate from my father both in domestic and in business affairs ... to the outside world, Carlo Verdi must be one thing and Giuseppe Verdi another.' When his mother died on 28 June Verdi was grief-stricken.

Having invested some of the profits of her years of singing and teaching in a business in Florence, Peppina always kept separate accounts, from which she contributed generously to many charities. She was a great support to Verdi and there is no doubt at all about the depth of feeling in their relationship, shown in the intimate letters she wrote when they were apart while he was preparing for the *premières* of his next two operas *Il trovatore* and *La traviata*. For instance, when he left her in Leghorn in January 1853, she wrote:

I confess my weakness, but this separation has been, for me, more painful than all the others. Without you I am a body without a soul. I am different (and I think you are, too) from those people who have need of frequent separations to revive their affection. I would stay with you for years and years, without boredom or satiety. On the contrary, now, after we've been together for a long time, without leaving each other for a moment, I feel our separation more keenly, although you give me reason to hope it will be brief.

She was not at all well, which may be why Verdi did not want to expose her to the tumult of the pre-production chaos during which, as usual, he had to conduct rehearsals and negotiate with the management over a host of details, while finishing off the orchestration of the score. At any rate she longed to be back amongst the peace of Sant' Agata, where she would curl up in an armchair in the corner of the room listening to him working out his compositions, occasionally interpolating her comments: 'That's beautiful'—'That's not'—'Stop'—'Repeat that'—'That's original.'

It was obviously a great sadness to her that she could not have children by him 'since God, perhaps, wishes to punish us for my sins, in depriving me of any legitimate joy before I die', but it is indicative of their relationship that she feared he might have a child by another woman. Indeed when in Venice with Piave for *Rigoletto* Verdi *did* flirt with a certain 'Angel' who later wrote to him *poste restante* at Cremona proposing to

Sant' Agata, a view across Verdi's estate. A photograph

Strepponi at the
beginning of her career,
Trieste 1835

Strepponi in 1845. Bust
by P. Tenerani (Villa
Verdi di Sant' Agata)

pay him a visit. Piave's reputation for womanising prompted Peppina to call him *Gran Diavolo* (Big Devil) and to instruct Verdi to tell him 'to show his erotic zeal with friends who resemble himself'. It was not to be the last time that there was to be a question-mark about Verdi's relationships with other women.

The question has to be asked: why did Verdi and Giuseppina live together for so long before marrying in 1859? Why did they risk the public hostility and scandal which marriage ten years earlier could have avoided? All answers are pure speculation since there is no direct evidence. Giuseppina did tell a Florentine friend that Verdi had vowed to Margherita on her death bed that he would never remarry, but there is no evidence to support this explanation. Some writers have suggested that Verdi's lack of belief may have been a barrier to a church marriage (yet he married both Margherita and Giuseppina in church); others that after his first wife's death he had a superstitious fear that any wife of his might die; but most seem to have overlooked the more obvious explanation that both wanted to be absolutely sure before embarking upon a marriage. Through the sudden ending of his previous marriage Verdi had been terribly hurt; Giuseppina, having been badly treated in her affaire with Moriani, may well have felt the need to tread warily, perhaps also judging that, in view of past failures, she was not worthy of 'her Verdi'.

Whatever the explanation, they regarded it as a private matter, so it seems probable that Antonio Barezzi, Verdi's 'father' in all but name, came near to ending his relationship with them by suggesting that the union be legalised. His letter has not survived but Verdi's reply on 21 January 1852 is well-known:

Dearest Father-in-law, After waiting such a long time, I hardly thought I would receive from you a letter so cold, and containing, if I am not mistaken, so many wounding phrases. If this letter had not been signed Antonio Barezzi, whom I wish to think of as my benefactor, I should have replied most strongly or not have replied at all. But since it is signed by that name which I shall always consider it my duty to respect, I shall do everything possible to persuade you that I do not merit such a reproof ...

Yet Verdi, in fact, reveals nothing. His letter is a masterpiece of the art of saying the maximum while disclosing the minimum:

In my house there lives a lady, free and independent, who, like myself, prefers a solitary life, and who has a fortune capable of satisfying all her needs. Neither I nor she is obliged to account to anyone for our actions. But who know what our relations are? What affairs? What ties? What rights I have over her or she over me. Who knows whether she is my wife or not? ... I will say this to you, however: in my house she is entitled to as much respect as myself, more even. And no one is allowed to forget that, for any reason. And finally she has every right, both because of her conduct and her character, to that consideration she habitually shows to others.

Apparently Barezzi accepted either the rebuke or the explanation for, when Léon Escudier, impresario of the Paris Opéra, came to Sant' Agata the following summer to present Verdi with the cross of the Légion d'Honneur, Barezzi was present, taking every opportunity to speak of his former *protégé* with tears in his eyes 'to the great despair of the Maestro, who,

Verdi in pensive mood, 1845

Salvatore Cammarano (1801–52), the librettist of several Verdi operas, including, most notably, *Il trovatore*

tired of the struggle, gave up trying to make him be quiet'. Verdi was overwhelmed with emotion at the honour of this decoration, which Barezzi promptly begged to be allowed to borrow, rushing off to show it proudly round Busseto.

Whatever the local inhabitants may have thought of Verdi's private life, there seems little doubt that the peace and security of life at Sant' Agata with Peppina provided an environment conducive to the growth of his musical creativity. Before they moved to Paris for the winter in 1851–2, he had already started work on *Il trovatore*, for which, only a month after the *première* of *Rigoletto*, Cammarano had provided an outline libretto based on Antonio Garcia Gutiérrez's play *El Trovador*. If Verdi had hoped to produce an opera full of exciting and bold innovation to follow *Rigoletto*, the rambling and unwieldy nature of the Spanish text and Cammarano's basic conservatism were to work against him. Verdi wrote to him on 4 April 1851:

You don't say a word about whether or not you like this drama. I suggested it to you because it seemed to me to offer fine theatrical effects and above all something original and out of the ordinary. If you didn't share my opinion, why didn't you propose another plot? ... If in the opera there were neither cavatinas, duets, trios, choruses, finales, etc. and the whole work consisted, let's say, of a single number I should find that all the more right and proper.

Verdi suggested changing to another plot altogether: 'I have ready another subject which is simple and tender and almost ready-made you might say.' It does not seem at all likely that this was, as has been suggested, *La Dame aux camélias* (later to become *La traviata*). Anyway Cammarano decided to persevere with *Il trovatore*.

Returning in March to Busseto, while waiting for the libretto from Cammarano, Verdi corresponded with Piave about the opera they had agreed to write for the carnival season of 1853 at La Fenice. In July, however, he was thunderstruck to read in a 'stupid theatrical journal' of Cammarano's death, for not only had he thereby lost a librettist but also a dearly loved friend. When he heard that the widow had been left in somewhat straitened circumstances, he paid her six hundred ducats (instead of the agreed five hundred). Cammarano had written almost the whole opera but Verdi's Neapolitan friend Cesare de Sanctis arranged for Leone Emanuele Bardare, a young poet, to finish it, in particular filling out the part of Leonora at Verdi's request.

The difficulties that present-day opera-goers find in the story of *Il trovatore* arise from the complexity of the original play, in which much of the action takes place off-stage, between the scenes, so that, for example, the entire first scene of the opera is taken up with a soldier recounting to his fellows 'the story so far'. This was the Romantic Age when stories of high melodrama were hugely successful and, at the same time, violence and sudden death were very much a part of Italian life. So audiences then would not have found the idea of a gipsy throwing a baby into a fire (even the wrong one by mistake) as absurd as many do today. Although the opera is full of brilliant melodies, its real distinction lies in the character of the gipsy Azucena.

Verdi considered her conflicting emotions of maternal and filial love to be the heart of the opera, emphasising to Cammarano that 'this woman's two great passions, her love for Manrico [whom she has brought up as her son] and her wild desire to avenge her mother [burnt at the stake by Count Luna], must be sustained to the end. When Manrico is dead, her feeling of revenge overwhelms her, and in the utmost agitation she cries [to the Count of Luna who has had Manrico executed]: "Yes, he was your brother ... Fool! ... Mother, you are avenged!" '

The opera had not been written on commission, but after negotiations with the Teatro San Carlo at Naples had failed, the *première* was arranged for the Teatro Apollo in Rome, now

The interior of the Teatro Apollo in Rome. Drawing by Bonamore

Pope Pius IX (Pio Nono) returns to Rome, 12 April 1850 (Mary Evans)

an occupied city since Pio Nono had been restored by French troops in April 1850. A balanced view of the city under the clerical regime enforced by the French is given in a letter from the historian Luigi Carlo Farini to Gladstone in December 1852:

The finances are ruined; commerce and traffic at the very lowest ebb; smuggling has sprung to life again ... taxes and rates are imposed in abundance, without rule or measure. There is neither public nor private safety; no moral authority, no real army, no railroads, no telegraphs. Studies are neglected; there is not a breath of liberty, not a hope of tranquil life; two foreign armies; a permanent state of siege, atrocious acts of revenge, factions raging, universal discontent; such is the Papal Government at the present day.

Verdi arrived in Rome, rehearsing *Trovatore* during the day while working on *Traviata* in his rooms at night: needless to say the pressure brought on his sore throat again, and rheumatism in his arm. At the first-night on 19 January 1853, *Il trovatore* was hailed as a masterpiece, the third act finale and the whole of the fourth act being encored. It was soon being given all over Europe and in many parts of the world, just as fast as Ricordi could distribute the scores. Barrel organs and street bands began to churn out the many tunes, including Azucena's 'Stride la vampa' and the 'Miserere' from the final act. Several contemporary critics complained that Verdi was ruining the art of *bel canto* by writing almost impossible parts for the singers (the opera is full of trills, high notes and passages which many singers find difficult to sing well), while others objected to the violence and gloom; but the *Gazzetta musicale* declared that Verdi deserved this splendid triumph since the music was 'heavenly'.

Returning from Rome, Verdi found two changes at Busseto: his father had become seriously ill and Muzio had left to become Director of the Théâtre-Italien in Brussels. Those at Sant' Agata were used to change of a less important kind since there were continual building alterations and additions. Peppina once wrote to Clarina Maffei: 'I cannot tell you how often during the building operations beds, wardrobes and furniture danced from room to room. It is enough to say that except for the kitchen, the cellar and the stables, we have slept and eaten our meals in every corner of the house.'

With such a short time until the *première* of *La traviata* Verdi concentrated all his attention on the opera. One political development must have distracted him. On the 6 February,

Rosina Penco (1823–94), the first Leonora in *Il trovatore*. Drawing by J. Pound

Giuseppe Mazzini (1805–72), an outstanding figure of the Risorgimento. It has been said that his philosophy was 'not only political, but deeply social, aiming at human redemption on a religious and moral basis, at liberty and at justice'. Drawing by G. Castagnola

Mazzini organised a disastrous attempt to capture the Milan fortress held by twelve thousand Austrians. Many of the members of his secret societies failed to appear on the day, the public did not respond to his appeal for a general insurrection, the Austrians exacted heavy penalties from the city, and most republicans, realising that such outbreaks achieved nothing, began to unite behind the movement for a united Italy under Vittorio Emanuele of Piedmont, the only north Italian state independent of Austria. If the event did not affect Verdi much, Muzio was not so fortunate. His opera *Claudia* was produced at the Teatro Carcano, Milan, on the day following the uprising, after which the Austrians closed the theatres.

Verdi had been most struck by a performance of the play *La Dame aux camélias* he had seen in Paris during the winter of 1851–2 but he did not select this for his next opera until the end of 1852. Dumas' central character, Marguerite Gautier, was based on the famous Parisian courtesan, Marie Duplessis, with whom Dumas, like Liszt and many others, had been involved before she died at the age of twenty-three in April 1847.

A typical Parisian *soirée* of the kind depicted in *La Dame aux camélias*. Etching by A. Hervieu, 1835 (from Frances Trollope's *Paris and the Parisians*, Vol. II, London 1836)

Verdi in 1853

She was called the Lady of the Camelias in the novel because she always wore white camelias except for five days in every month when they were red. Having promised to become Armand's mistress she gives him a red camelia, instructing him to return when the flowers are white for 'you cannot always carry out treaties the day you sign them'. As Julian Budden has put it, 'the French have a delicate way of expressing the cruder facts of life'. Such realistic details however disappear in Dumas' play and Verdi's opera. This lady of the *demi-monde* (a term Dumas himself invented to describe mistresses who were kept in style but not received

Marie Duplessis
(1824–47), the courtesan
of whom Liszt said 'I
know not what strange
chord of antic elegy
vibrates in my heart
when I remember her.'

into 'Society') was transformed in Verdi's opera into Violetta, who leaves the gay, social life of Paris to live in the country with young Alfredo Germont, until his father, unbeknown to his son, persuades her that she is ruining his and his sister's lives. Alfredo only learns the true reason for her desertion in time to be reunited with her just before she dies of consumption. Violetta must have stirred many memories of Margherita's early death and Giuseppina's previous life; so it is not surprising that the music depicts her with great tenderness, her bright and taxing *coloratura* part when she is shown in the fashionable world of the first act contrasting movingly with the simpler, elegiac melodies of the later scenes with Alfredo in the country and on her death-bed.

Verdi and Piave were most courageous to tackle such a scandalous subject, but the first productions, in an attempt to lessen the force of the opera as a comment on contemporary life, dressed it in the costumes of the reign of Louis XIV thereby making a nonsense of the entire basis of the plot. The impresario Lasina made Verdi's opposition to the plan absolutely clear in a memorandum of 11 January 1853: 'The Signor Maestro Verdi desires, demands and begs that the costumes for his opera *La traviata* should remain those of the present day.' But Verdi very much against his will had later to agree to the period being put back in time. He was also implacably opposed to the soprano Fanny Salvini-Donatelli singing the rôle of Violetta. Piave stated to the management: 'He insists with renewed firmness that to sing *Traviata* one must be young, have a graceful figure and sing with passion.' Piave admitted also that he had not warned the Maestro of the poor quality of the Venetian company. Verdi received an anonymous letter advising him that, unless the singers were changed, the *première* would be a disaster. 'I know, I know, and I'll prove it to you', he said despairingly, even threatening to cancel the contract. None of the singers could be replaced so, after only thirteen weeks of rehearsals, *La traviata* was first performed at La Fenice on 6 March 1853. Before he had seen the reviews Verdi wrote to Tito Ricordi: 'I am sorry to have to give you sad news, but I cannot conceal the truth. *La traviata* was a fiasco. Let's not enquire into the reasons. That's what happened. Farewell, Farewell;' and to Muzio: '*La traviata* was a fiasco; my fault or the singers'? Time alone will tell.' To Angelo Mariani, the future conductor of *Aroldo*, he revealed that the audience had laughed at the plump soprano Fanny Salvini-Donatelli's attempt to portray convincingly a lady dying of consumption, although she nevertheless received

82

Fanny Salvini-Donatelli who created the rôle of Violetta in *La traviata*, and whose plain, dumpy figure was so in contrast to that of the beautiful, consumptive Marie Duplessis. Engraving by A. Bedetti

more applause than anyone else. The critics however were more fair, some reserving judgement until the opera should be better sung. A second production was mounted over a year later in Venice's smaller Teatro San Benedetto by Antonio Gallo, the violinist turned impresario, with tremendous success. It soon became the favourite opera of its day as performances were given all over Italy and Europe. Violetta was performed on this occasion by the young and pretty Maria Spezia, who was *so* frail that Piave had been greatly concerned for her health during an earlier performance of *I due Foscari*.

La traviata is undoubtedly one of Verdi's supreme achievements and remains one of the world's most popular operas. Its domestic subject, so closely related to his own life, enabled Verdi to pour his soul into the music that contains such a wealth of unforgettable melody. Each of the characters is finely drawn and, most notable of all, the unity of the entire work is maintained by the way that, in the words of Charles Osborne, 'its separate numbers arise from and merge into the general melodic background'.

Verdi had written to Contessa Maffei after the *première* of *Il trovatore*: 'People say the opera is too sad, and that there are too many deaths in it. But, after all, death is all there is in life. What else is there?' Verdi's three middle-period operas all share a preoccupation with gloom and horror, violence and hatred, despair and death, at the very time when he might have been expected, because of the happiness of his personal life, to be contemplating a brighter philosophy.

The final scene of *La traviata*. Detail from the title page of the original vocal score

The interior of the Paris
Opéra, 1854 (Mary
Evans)

The new ponds laid in
the Bois de Boulogne
during Napoleon III's
rebuilding of Paris

Chapter 6
Viva Italia!

'I am a son of the people, and more proud of this than of any title on earth!'—Garibaldi.

During the spring and summer of 1853 Verdi immersed himself in the countryside and farming, rising at dawn to go into the woods and fields amongst the peasants and the animals, taking an ever-growing interest in the produce and the running of his estate. Yet opera was still never far from his mind for throughout the summer he corresponded regularly with the Venetian playwright Antonio Somma about a libretto for *King Lear*. After highly detailed discussions Somma produced and was paid for the *Lear* libretto, but by then Verdi had started work on *Les Vêpres siciliennes* (*The Sicilian Vespers*) for the Paris Opéra.

After toying with the idea of spending the winter in Naples, Verdi and Giuseppina travelled to Paris just after they had celebrated the composer's fortieth birthday. Napoleon III had set out to lead the France of the Second Empire into the Industrial Age by reorganizing industry, banking and transportation; but perhaps his most spectacular project was the rebuilding of the capital. On his arrival Verdi found that, to enable the surveyors to triangulate and map the city, wooden towers had been set up at many street corners to the considerable amusement of the populace. Newspapers printed cartoons showing possible uses for the towers—tightrope walkers carrying messages between them and cannon firing the surveyors up to their lofty posts.

Verdi soon had to turn his attention to *Les Vêpres siciliennes*. In his three previous operas he had evolved a close-knit, swiftly-moving form in which the exploration of the characters was of supreme importance. The tradition of the Paris Opéra was completely different—grand spectacle was *de rigueur*—five acts, a ballet, full-scale choruses, elaborate scenery and effects, magnificent costumes and lavish presentation. The chief exponents of this tradition were Meyerbeer and his librettist

Giacomo Meyerbeer
(1791–1864)

Sophie Cruvelli
(1826–1907), the first
Hélène in Les Vêpres
siciliennes. Drawing by A.
Collette

Eugène Scribe with operas like *Les Huguenots*, containing scenes ranging from a ballet of ladies bathing in the river to a massacre lasting a whole act; *Robert le diable* with its ballet of decidedly dissolute nuns dancing in the graveyard; and *Le Prophète*, which had a ballet on roller skates, a coronation, and a bacchanalian banquet ending with an explosion that brought down all the scenery. No wonder that Verdi commented: 'A work for the Opéra is enough to fell a bull! Five hours of music. Phew!' In fact he hoped to capitalise on what was best in the tradition, and asked Scribe for 'a subject that is grandiose, impassioned and original; a *mise-en-scène* that is imposing and overwhelming'.

Scribe was twenty-two years older than Verdi and, as the fashionable author of countless scripts, was immensely rich. He based the libretto of *Les Vêpres* on one he had written for Donizetti's as yet unperformed *Le Duc d'Albe*. Scribe stated in various letters that he had informed the composer of this, but Verdi later expressed considerable surprise when the connection between the two libretti came to light. At any rate Scribe took an exasperatingly long time to finish it. The story is based on the Massacre of 1282 when the inhabitants of Palermo murdered the occupying French troops as the church bells were ringing for vespers. Verdi completed four of the five acts and rehearsals began, but after a few days the principal soprano, Sophie Cruvelli, suddenly disappeared without a word of explanation. Excitement and speculation was high (in London a farce was put on at the Strand Theatre called *Where's Cruvelli?*). Verdi wanted to give up and return to Italy and to *King Lear*, but just as suddenly Cruvelli reappeared, having apparently been away with her lover and future husband, Baron Vigier.

During the singer's absence one of Verdi's longest friendships came sadly to an end. Apparently Mme Appiani wrote to Giuseppina at Sant' Agata addressing her letter to 'Giuseppina Strepponi', which was of course technically correct. Certainly by 1857 Peppina was passing everywhere as Verdi's wife and signing her name as 'Giuseppina [or Josephine] Verdi', even though they were not married until 1859. In 1855 however 'the Verdis' obviously expected discretion and consideration from an old friend, so Giuseppina left the Maestro to write a brief, though not unkind, reply on her behalf, which nevertheless had the effect of terminating the correspondence and friendship.

Meanwhile relationships with Scribe and the management were deteriorating. Verdi now wrote on 3 January 1855 to

Napoleon III and the Empress Eugénie arriving at Windsor Castle on the occasion of their State Visit to Britain, April 1855 (Mary Evans)

Louis Crosnier, the Director of the Opéra, complaining in some detail about the text and Scribe's conduct:

It is both saddening and humiliating for me that M. Scribe is not taking the trouble to put right this fifth act, which everyone agrees in finding dull. I am not unware that M. Scribe has a thousand other things to do which perhaps he has more to heart than my opera! ... but if I could have had any suspicion of this sovereign indifference I would have stayed in my own country where, really, I was not doing so badly.

Verdi asked for many changes, and, although Crosnier would not grant his request to be released from his contract, obviously some agreement was reached since rehearsals dragged on.

It is ironic that in spite of all the contretemps surrounding its composition, the *première* of *Les Vêpres siciliennes* on 13 June 1855 during the *Exposition Universelle* was a splendid success, the opera being subsequently given fifty performances that

Queen Victoria and the Prince Consort arriving in Paris on the occasion of *their* State Visit to France, August 1855, when they attended the Exposition Universelle (Mary Evans)

season. Because of censorship difficulties it was translated in Italy under various titles, until six years later it was given the Italian title by which it is now generally known—*I vespri siciliani*. When Berlioz had seen it he wrote:

Without casting a slur on the merits of *Il trovatore* and so many other moving works of his, it must be agreed that in the *Vêpres* the penetrating intensity of melodic expression, the sumptuous variety, the judicious sobriety of the orchestration, the amplitude, the poetic sonority of his *morceaux d'ensemble*, the warm colours glowing everywhere and that sense of power, impassioned but slow to unfold, that is one of the characteristics of Verdi's genius, stamp the whole work with a grandeur, a sovereign majesty more marked than in the composer's previous creations.

Verdi remained in Paris for the summer and was there when Queen Victoria and Prince Albert arrived in August to repay the Emperor's visit to London and Windsor that had taken place in the spring. After spending some time at Saint Cloud, Victoria visited several times the *Exposition Universelle* in the glass-roofed Palais des Beaux Arts. With typically mid-nineteenth century taste the visitors strolled past the paintings by Ingres and Delacroix to linger in front of the vast canvasses by Decamps, Meissonier and Horace Vernet, even sitting down to admire the idealised portraits of the Imperial family by Winterhalter that bore little resemblance to their originals.

88

The Queen loved the Sèvres porcelain which she declared to be '*quite* magnificent'. Her boundless energy soon exhausted her retinue in the great heat of that summer, but she was delighted with Paris and its people, and wrote in her diary: 'Everything so gay, so bright, and though very hot, the air so clear and light. The absence of smoke keeps everything so white and bright, and this in Paris, with much gilding about the shops, shutters, etc., produces a brilliancy of effect which is quite incredible.'

Verdi's stay in Paris was not so pleasant, as he became embroiled in wrangles over the copyright of his scores. One of the reasons why earlier composers, like Rossini and Donizetti, had composed so many operas was that they were paid by the publisher only for the original, which then became public property after two years. With vastly improved communications and the growth of readily-printed musical scores making it possible for operas to be performed in other countries within a short time after publication, copyright laws and the payment of royalties to the composer and publisher were introduced. But these laws varied tremendously between countries, so that in the mid-nineteenth century 'pirated' editions and productions were a common hazard.

Verdi had to go twice to London to prevent unauthorised performances of *Il trovatore*. At the same time he was negotiating with Calzado, manager of the Théâtre-Italien in Paris, who was threatening to use 'pirated' editions unless the royalties were reduced; Verdi was eventually forced to institute a lawsuit, which he lost. He resented the fact that Tito Ricordi's Parisian agent was not looking after his interests, so he began a lengthy and often acrimonious correspondence with his publisher. Although Verdi had some cause for just complaint (for example, Ricordi had not withdrawn the first edition of *La traviata* as Verdi had requested since he had made several changes after the first unsuccessful production), there is no doubt that at the root of it all lay the composer's resentment that the publication of his compositions had allowed Ricordi to amass a colossal fortune.

On his return to Sant' Agata at the end of 1856 Verdi began to re-work *Stiffelio* in collaboration with Piave, turning it into *Aroldo*, the story of an English crusader, which was produced at Rimini in August 1857 with Mariani as conductor. More importantly, Verdi conducted a revival of *La traviata* in Venice in March 1856 which made such an impression that he agreed to write a new opera for the same theatre next season. Once again choosing a play by Antonio García Gutiérrez, author of

Tito Ricordi (1811–88). Drawing by Mancastropa

Antonio Somma the librettist of *Un ballo in maschera*

The soprano Maria Piccolomini (1834–99) in the title rôle in the first scene of *La traviata*. Painting by Daniele

El Trovador, Piave and Verdi completed *Simon Boccanegra* in ten months, during which time Verdi visited London and Paris to fight further copyright battles and supervise a French production of *Il trovatore*, which required the addition of ballet music.

While in Paris, finding communication with Piave in Italy extremely difficult, Verdi asked Giuseppe Montanelli, an exiled professor of law, to re-write parts of the libretto. *Simon Boccanegra* tells the story of a buccaneer turned Doge of Genoa who strives to create a united country, by reconciling the patrician and plebian factions. The *première* on 12 March 1857 was a flop. '*Boccanegra* was almost a greater fiasco in Venice than *Traviata*', wrote Verdi to Contessa Maffei. 'I thought I had done something fairly good, but now it seems I was mistaken.' A review in the *Gazzetta Privilegiata di Venezia* on 15 March pointed to some of the reasons for the opera's failure to capture the public imagination:

The music of *Boccanegra* is of the kind that does not make its effect immediately. It is very elaborate, written with the most exquisite craftsmanship and needs to be studied in all its details. From this it came about that on the first night it was not fully understood and led to some hasty judgments—judgments so bitter and hostile in the form in which they were expressed ... as to appear singular and strange to say the least. This first, unfavourable impression can be to some extent explained by the character of the music which is perhaps too heavy and severe, and by that mournful colour that dominated the score especially the prologue.

Verdi's audiences had come to expect melodic profusion from him, whereas in *Simon Boccanegra* there are long sections of accompanied recitative that were found to be excessive in a work of which the atmosphere is oppressively dark and gloomy throughout. Once Verdi's next opera, *Un ballo in maschera*, had appeared, *Simon Boccanegra* disappeared from the repertoire until the composer was persuaded to revise it over twenty years later.

During this time Verdi had not only continued his correspondence with Somma about *King Lear* but had even opened negotiations with the Neapolitan music critic Vincenzo Torelli to stage it at the Teatro San Carlo where Torelli was a partner. Having been strongly critical of Verdi, Torelli had been converted into one of his most fervent admirers. Verdi was convinced that they needed 'a really fine baritone for the rôle of King Lear' and 'a leading soprano, not a dramatic soprano, but a singer of expressive quality for Cordelia'. Having persuaded Maria Piccolomini to sing the

An original scenery sketch by Gerolamo Magnani for the revised version of *Simon Boccanegra* at La Scala in 1881

latter rôle when he was in Paris for his lawsuit in the summer of 1857, he appeared satisfied with the strong San Carlo company for the remaining rôles, and so signed a contract with the theatre to produce an unspecified opera there in January 1858.

However, as the San Carlo did not succeed in obtaining Piccolomini, Verdi vacillated in spite of Torelli's plea in a letter of 26 September 1857: 'Give us *King Lear*, for although some other time you may happen upon a better Cordelia, you will never have a better baritone, tenor or bass. Set your genius to work; I hear that *La traviata*—a true musico-social revolution—was composed in a very short time. I hope you will produce a second *Traviata* for us.' But Verdi was not to be persuaded and one can only conclude that he wanted an excuse to abandon the project. His much-quoted remark in 1896 when offering the libretto to the young Mascagni, who had already made his name with *Cavalleria Rusticana*, that 'the

Friends and conspirators surround Gustavus III in an illustration from the title page of a typical early pot-pourri based on Auber's *Gustave III ou Le bal masqué*, first given at the Paris Opéra in 1833 (Ateş Orga)

scene in which King Lear finds himself alone on the heath terrified me' shows how inadequate he considered himself to be to do justice to this monumental Shakespearian drama. It is above all an 'interior' drama—the probing of one man's mind—and this, coupled with the multiplicity of scenes, proved an almost insuperable obstacle to the production of an effective libretto and opera. Although Boito tried to rekindle his interest towards the end of his life, regrettably Verdi's *King Lear* was never to be.

Another libretto had therefore to be found for the San Carlo. Having spent much time looking through 'an infinite number of plays' to find something excitingly different, Verdi was forced by the pressures of time to choose a libretto by Scribe, *Gustave III ou Le bal masqué*, even though the story had been used by, amongst others, Auber and Mercadante (for *Il reggente*). Verdi himself had plenty of reservations about it: 'It's vast and grandiose; it's beautiful; but it too has conventional things in it like all operas—something I've always disliked and now find intolerable.'

In their discussions over *King Lear* Verdi found that Somma.

though a successful playwright, needed to be constantly instructed in the basic rules of writing for an opera. In spite of this drawback, Somma translated and reduced Scribe's text, though he constantly refused to allow his name to appear on the libretto. As it is the real-life story of the assassination of the Swedish King at a masked ball in 1792, difficulties were to be expected with the *censura*, but it was hoped to overcome these by changing the names of people and places as in *Rigoletto*; yet when Verdi arrived in Naples in the New Year of 1858 he discovered that the censor would not even then permit the opera to be staged.

Once again the reasons lay in the ever-changing and extremely tense political situation. After the Crimean War, France's ascendancy in Europe had been re-established, while Italy had gained a voice in the Councils of Europe through Count Camillo Cavour's foresight in sending Piedmontese troops to fight on behalf of the allies. When Cavour merged the groups working for independence in a movement that rejected Mazzini and his policy of violent revolution, England and France let it be known that they would support the unification of Italy under Vittorio Emanuele of Piedmont, to whom Manin delivered his famous dictum: 'Make Italy and I am with you; if not, no!' The Austrian Emperor, Franz Josef, tried to redeem the situation by visiting Milan and Venice to

Little Dorrit watches Mr Sparkler's accident in a gondola in Venice. Illustration by H.K. Browne from the original edition of Charles Dickens' novel, *Little Dorrit* (London 1857)

The attempt of 14 January 1858 on Napoleon III's life. An artist's impression, *L'Illustration*, 23 January 1858

institute some reforms, but his reception in the Po valley was cold. At Padua the Mayor in the first carriage urged hostile onlookers to cheer the Emperor and Empress in the third carriage. To his chagrin the crowd dutifully cried: 'Viva la terza carozza!' ('Long live the third carriage!'). The Contessa Maffei and her social circle spurned, and even arranged duels against, any who attended social functions organised by Radetsky's replacement, the Archduke Maximilian.

A good picture of the heavy hand of Austria that had lain on the country for years is given in Charles Dickens' *Little Dorrit*. Although it is supposedly set earlier, it draws heavily on Dickens' own journey to Italy in the early 1850s:

They would come to whole towns of palaces, whose proper inmates were banished, and which were all changed into barracks: troops of idle soldiers leaning out of the state-windows, where their accoutrements hung drying on the marble architecture, and showing to the mind like hosts of rats who were (happily) eating away the props of the edifices that supported them, and must soon with them, be smashed on the heads of the other swarms of soldiers, and the swarms of priests, and the swarms of spies, who were all the ill-looking population left to be ruined, in the streets below.

The result was that the censors became more repressive. When, on 14 January 1858, the very day Verdi arrived in Naples, Felice Orsini and some confederates, all of them followers of Mazzini, failed to assassinate Napoleon III in a bomb attack on his carriage outside the Paris Opéra, the chances of a libretto about regicide being passed became even more remote, particularly since people had also not forgotten the assassination attempt on King Ferdinand of Naples only a year before.

The San Carlo management produced an alternative libretto set in fourteenth century Florence, which met all the censor's objections; but Verdi quite rightly considered that the words and music did not match and, what was worse, the replacement libretto made nonsense of the entire opera. A banquet had been substituted for the masked ball and so, wrote Verdi, 'everyone recognizes everyone else; thus the stage play is lost and nothing which is said has any sense.' The management sued Verdi in an attempt to force him to release the music; Verdi counter-sued, thus beginning a lawsuit that created a great scandal, in which most Neapolitans sided with the composer, gathering outside his window to cheer him. Under government pressure the matter was settled out of court, the original contract was dissolved and Verdi agreed to stage *Simon Boccanegra* which had not previously been seen in Venice.

It was while they were in Naples that Verdi and Giuseppina met the caricaturist Melchiorré Delfico, whose cartoons of the 'Bear of Busseto' were hugely enjoyed by their original. Delfico's drawings show that Giuseppina had with her her new dog Loulou, brought from Venice by Piave on the Maestro's instructions. Verdi began negotiations with the Roman impresario Vincenzo Jacovacci to stage *La vendetta in domino* (the title he had given to Scribe's *Gustave III*) at the Teatro Apollo provided the Papal censor's approval could be obtained. It was Donizetti's brother-in-law, Vasselli, who agreed to negotiate with the censor on Verdi's behalf. After a summer spent on the farm at Sant' Agata, during which the conductor Mariani joined him for some weeks of shooting, the libretto was finally approved by the Papal authorities on condition that the setting should not be in Europe. In the end Verdi and Somma chose seventeenth-century Boston. There seems little doubt that Verdi was quite satisfied with this, since, being unaware of the Salem witch-hunts, he appears incorrectly to have thought it was somewhat like contemporary Restoration England, well-known in Italy through such works as Scott's *Peveril of the Peak*. At any rate the libretto was altered to fit this new setting and the opera re-entitled *Un ballo in maschera* (*A masked ball*).

When Verdi and Giuseppina arrived in Rome in January 1859 rumours that Cavour had secretly met Napoleon III to

Verdi and Loulou
greeting the Neapolitan
librettist Baron
Genovesi. A cartoon by
Melchiorre Delfico,
1858–59

'Viva Verdi!', 1859.
L'Illustrazione Italiana, 3
February 1901 (Julian
Budden)

plan war on Austria were everywhere—rumours that were
reinforced by Vittorio Emanuele's speech declaring that 'we
cannot remain insensitive to the cry of grief that has reached
us from so many parts of Italy'. The patriotic feelings thus
stirred up were given vent at the *première* of *Ballo* on 17
February for when the audience shouted 'Viva Verdi!' Italians
began to realise that this was an acrostic for **V**ittorio
Emanuele **Re D'I**talia, so that it was soon being painted on
walls, shouted in the streets and displayed on banners.

The opera was also applauded for its intrinsic merit. The
rôle of Riccardo (Gustavo), excellently given at the *première* by
Gaetano Fraschini, is a most varied tenor rôle—one moment
he is the elegant courtier, another moment light-hearted, then
passionate, while in the scene with the fortune-teller Ulrica
(Mme Arvidson) his singing has to match his sailor's disguise
until he greets Ulrica's prophecy of his death with the laugh of
a cynically-amused aristocrat. Oscar is, for Verdi, a
considerable step forwards with its sparkling gaiety and wit. It

Gaetano Fraschini
(1816–87) in his earlier
rôle of Foresto in Verdi's
Attila

is this blend of the comic and tragic 'in Shakespeare's manner' that gives *Ballo* its particular distinction. Renato's well-known aria 'Eri tu' ('It was you') throws the dark and light sides of the opera into stark relief, for it is at this moment that the faithful servant becomes the menacing conspirator. *Un ballo in maschera* with its 'classical poise and balance' is not, however, a work of great innovation. It is perhaps best summed up in a sub-sequent review by the critic Filippo Filippi in *La Perseveranza*:

In *Un ballo in maschera*, having rejected convention and formula, having assigned to each character his own particular language and having rendered the dramatic situation with evident effectiveness, in fact having moulded the drama, Verdi can take his seat between the past and the future and turning round to each of the two sides can say to one party: 'Do you want tunes, ideas, proportions, beginning, a middle, continuation and an end? Do you want rhythm, phrasing, pure music? You have it and to spare: And you others, gentlemen of the future, do you want general colouring of the drama, faithful interpretation of the words, freedom from hackneyed and conventional forms? Do you want banality banished and in its place the new and the elegant? Do you want the orchestra and the stage to be like a single statue? and a kind of aesthetic pantheism to prevail everywhere? Help yourselves; there is plenty for all your needs.'

Both before and after *Ballo* there is a two year gap (the same time span in which Verdi had earlier composed *Rigoletto*, *Trovatore* and *Traviata*). The pace of composition was slowing down not only because he needed longer to compose an opera, but also because he was becoming increasingly involved in domestic affairs and in politics. On 22 August 1859 Verdi and Streppони were married in Savoy, which was at that time part of Italy, at Collonges-sous-Salève by an Abbé Mermillod whom they had brought with them from Geneva. The Abbé sent 'the local parish-priest out for a walk perhaps so that He [*sic*] would not have to share the fee', as Verdi drily commented.

In the spring of 1859 the Austrians sent an ultimatum to Piedmont instructing them to disband their army, so the French came to Italy's aid. In the war that followed, with its major battles of Magenta and Solferino proving indecisive, the main hero was Vittorio Emanuele, much to Napoleon's annoyance who, finding himself out of the limelight, concluded the Treaty of Villafranca with Austria. Although the effect was to create a Kingdom of some of the North Italian states, Austria was to retain Venice. Verdi believed that it meant 'that we can never hope for anything from any foreigner of whatever nation'.

98

Detail from the title page of the original vocal score of *Un ballo in maschera* (*cf* the illustration on p. 92 from Auber's opera on the same subject)

When Parma voted in a plebiscite for union with Piedmont, Verdi was elected by Busseto as a delegate to the Assembly, from which he was one of five men selected to bear its homage to Vittorio Emanuele in Turin. He also visited Cavour, whom he called 'the Prometheus of our nation'. When it became apparent that Savoy and Nice were to be ceded to France as the price for French aid, Garibaldi and his Redshirts ('The Thousand') carried out their amazing capture of Sicily and Naples, forcing Cavour to dispatch the Piedmontese army under General Cialdini 'to absorb' the guerillas so that Vittorio Emanuele should be seen to be the victor. Writing to Mariani, Verdi said of Garibaldi and Cialdini: 'Those are the composers! And what operas! What finales! To the sound of guns!' In fact, Mariani and Verdi arranged to buy some guns to equip the Busseto volunteers but they were not needed. Garibaldi, never able to forgive the King for failing to appear at the farewell review, turned down all proffered rewards and retired to the island of Caprera taking with him only a bag of seed corn. Giuseppina called him 'the purest and greatest hero since the world was created'.

Garibaldi's Redshirts landing at Calabria, 19 August 1860. *Illustrated London News* (Mary Evans)

Opposite
Verdi as a member of the delegation of the Assembly meeting Vittorio Emmanuele II in 1859. Drawing by Edoardo Matania, *L'Illustrazione Italiana*, 3 February 1901 (Julian Budden)

When the elections to the new Italian Parliament took place, Verdi was persuaded by Cavour to stand, much to the consternation of the other candidate, a local lawyer, Giovanni Minghelli-Vanni, who had been assured by Giuseppina that the Maestro would refuse any nomination. Verdi was of course elected, but declared after his term of office that 'there were in fact not 450, but 449 members, since, as a Deputy, Verdi was non-existent'. He voted only as Cavour did, his sole active participation being in a project for the government to subsidise the main theatres—a plan which disappeared with Cavour's sudden death in 1861. Verdi was heartbroken at the loss to Italy and, unable to bring himself to attend the funeral in Turin, he organised a memorial service in Busseto where, he confessed, he 'wept like a child'. Verdi's contribution to the new Italian nationalism was not to be in Parliament for which he had always considered himself ill-suited. Although he remained a Deputy until the next elections in 1865, he rarely attended after Cavour's death, devoting himself to his home and his music.

Chapter 7
The Force Of Destiny

'The Wagner of our allies'—Hans von Bülow

Enrico Tamberlick
(1820–89)

It may surprise us that the venue for Verdi's next opera *première* was to be St Petersburg, but it would not have seemed particularly unusual to his contemporaries who knew that many Italian artists and musicians had long been an important part of the Russian city's cultural life. Indeed, Italian dominance of the opera there had only recently been challenged by German and Russian composers, and it was the opera house's leading tenor, Enrico Tamberlick, who had written to Verdi suggesting that he might compose an opera for Russia.

The educated classes in mid-nineteenth century Russia were at home with European civilisation, which is why the arts flourished in the major cities, even though serfdom and poverty provoked much unrest amongst the peasants. After the failures of the Crimean War, Alexander II had become Tsar in 1856 and started some social reforms. In the very year in which the Verdis arrived in Russia the serfs were emancipated; although in practice, since the land they were given was not enough to live off and no peasant could leave his village without permission, they had to continue to work for their former masters at whatever rate they chose to pay. They were, therefore, little better off and felt cheated that their liberation had failed to bring them any benefit. This discontent was to culminate in the assassination of the Tsar in 1881, but while Verdi was in Russia in 1862 there was still an atmosphere of euphoria while Alexander's social reforms were being put into effect.

Tamberlick had to send his son Achille to persuade Verdi to write another opera for, in the two years since the *première* of *Ballo,* the composer had left music on one side, going so far as to state in a letter to Piave on 2 September 1859: 'As you know I am the complete countryman. I hope I have bidden farewell to the muses and that I shall never again feel the temptation to take up my pen.' Certainly Verdi could, and did, cut himself off from music at Sant' Agata. Friends who came to visit were often warned beforehand that music was not discussed there and that if they attempted to play the piano they would probably find it out of tune or even that some of the strings were missing. Verdi was to write to the critic Filippo Filippi on 21 May 1869 explaining:

In my house there is hardly any music; I have never been to a music library nor to a publisher's to study a piece of music. I am familiar with some of the best contemporary operas not from having read them but from having heard them in the theatre. In all this there is a definite policy as you will doubtless realise. I repeat that of all composers past and present I am the least erudite ... I refer to erudition, not musical knowledge. In that respect I should lie if I said that I had not studied hard and thoroughly in my youth. Indeed it is for this reason that I have a hand strong enough to bend the notes to my will.

His hard early training and wealth of experience were now to be used again, for he eventually agreed to Tamberlick's suggestion. His first choice of subject was Victor Hugo's *Ruy Blas* which had already inspired an overture by Mendelssohn, but this story of a valet, who becomes the lover of the Empress and subsequently Prime Minister, elevated the common man too highly for the taste of Tsarist Russia, so Verdi selected instead a play by the Spaniard, the Duke of Rivas, *Don Alvaro o La Fuerza del Sino (Don Alvaro or The force of destiny)*. Angel Perez de Saavedra, Duke of Rivas, had risen to high office in the Spanish Government after much time spent in exile in France, Malta and Portugal for his liberal opinions. He was also a great Romantic poet and historian, a fervent admirer of Victor Hugo and Sir Walter Scott. Verdi wrote to Léon Escudier 'the play is powerful, singular and truly vast; I like it very much'; but he also expressed some doubts: 'I don't know if the public will find it as I do, but it is certainly something quite out of the ordinary.' He was right to feel these reservations since the opera's libretto multiplies the coincidences of the original play so that the end result is a highly implausible story.

Throughout the summer of 1861 he worked with Piave on the opera. This was to be the last new opera he would work on with the man he had harried and instructed for so many years and who was, at this time, happily married and settled, thanks to Verdi, as resident stage director at La Scala, Milan. By the end of October Verdi was able to announce to Tamberlick:

St Petersburg, a tour of the Church of St Nicholas. Engraving, 1857

'This accursed *Forza del destino* is practically finished apart from the orchestration, which is no great matter. Any quarter of an hour serves to get on with this work. I write to you in fret and fury and must run back to my martyrdom.' It is probable that he had only agreed to write an opera because the extensive alterations to Sant' Agata had left him somewhat short of money.

At the beginning of 1862 he journeyed with Giuseppina to Russia, following in the footsteps of Robert and Clara Schumann who had toured Russia in 1844. They travelled on the recently completed railway from Paris to St Petersburg, where they were immediately struck by many strange sights—the churches painted green, wooden pavements, the prohibition against smoking in the streets, the flat, silent landscape, and above all the cold. Verdi was to write to Tamberlick later when they had left Russia: 'Now I understand the meaning of *cold* ... If I could believe in another world, an inferno of ice as Papa Dante says, I would begin tomorrow to recite the *rosary* and *miserere* and ask for pardon for all my sins committed and uncommitted.'

In fact, Giuseppina had taken precautions to make their visit as pleasant as possible by ordering in advance 100 bottles of light Bordeaux dinner wines, 20 bottles of fine Bordeaux, 20 bottles of champagne, as well as rice, *maccheroni*, and cheese fine enough to keep her temperamental husband in good spirits. She was well aware of the privileges of the rich, describing to their mutual friend Count Opprandino Arrivabene how the poor coachmen had to freeze for hours outside waiting for their rich masters 'guzzling in beautifully warm apartments'.

Unfortunately the *première* of *Forza* had to be postponed until the following autumn owing to the illness of the soprano, for whom no substitute could immediately be found. The Verdis travelled to London via Berlin, as Verdi had reluctantly agreed to represent Italy at the 1862 London Exhibition. Sterndale Bennett for England, Auber for France and, oddly enough, Meyerbeer for Germany were all contributing orchestral pieces, so Verdi decided to compose a choral work. His *Inno delle Nazioni* (*Hymn of the Nations*) was to a text by Arrigo Boito, who had been recommended to him by Contessa Maffei. Boito was the son of a Polish countess and an Italian miniature painter, and, with his friend Franco Faccio, had won a travelling scholarship from the Milan Conservatory. They had just arrived in Paris where they were determined to bring Italy into the mainstream of European culture. Verdi presented Boito with a watch, adjuring him to make good use of time. Verdi's cantata included the English National Anthem, *La*

Verdi in a troika, St Petersburg 1862

The London Exhibition, 1862 (Mary Evans)

Marseillaise and an Italian nationalistic song. It was either this use of revolutionary songs (the *Marseillaise* was not then in use as the French national anthem), or the jealousy of the Italian conductor Michael Costa, or that Verdi should not have written a choral work, that caused the *Inno* to be rejected on the grounds that there was not enough time to learn it. Verdi commented in a letter to *The Times* that twenty-five days were enough to learn a whole opera.

A performance was arranged at Her Majesty's Theatre on 24 May, Queen Victoria's birthday. It was quite well received, although *The Times* did not like 'the somewhat bombastic lines of the poetaster [Boito] whom it has been the fortune of the popular Italian composer to immortalise'. In fact, in the future they were to achieve immortality *together* through *Otello* and *Falstaff*.

Verdi and Giuseppina returned for the summer to Sant' Agata where Peppina's little dog Loulou died—she was heartbroken and always kept an oil-painting of the dog in her room, while Verdi had 'To the memory of one of my most faithful friends' inscribed in marble on the grave. Peppina's sister, Barberina, a lifelong invalid who was thought to be dying in Cremona, came to be nursed at Sant' Agata during the same summer—in the event she was to survive them both, dying at a ripe old age during the First World War.

In the autumn the Verdis returned to St Petersburg for the *première* of *La forza del destino* on 10 November 1862, when it was given a fairly good reception. In the *Journal de St Petersbourg* one writer declared: 'It is our opinion that *La forza del destino*, of all Verdi's works, is the most complete, both in terms of its inspiration and the rich abundance of its melodic invention, and in those of its musical development and orchestration.' The Tzar attended the fourth performance and bestowed on the composer the Order of Saint Stanislas, a decoration rare for an artist. The Nationalist Party, however, staged a hostile demonstration, probably in protest at the 22,000 roubles Verdi was paid (Russian composers received 500 roubles for an opera). Verdi himself was dissatisfied with the work (particularly the dénouement) and in 1869 revised it for a production at La Scala with the help of Antonio Ghislanzoni, editor of the Milanese *Gazzetta Musicale*, the future librettist of *Aida*. In particular the ending was altered 'to avoid all those dead bodies' as Verdi put it, so Alvaro's suicide is replaced by christian submission to the force of destiny.

Tsar Alexander II (1818–81). Engraving by D.J. Pound (Mary Evans)

La forza del destino is especially distinguished by two almost diametrically opposed aspects. Leonora, having lost her lover Don Alvaro, who had inadvertently killed her father, comes to a monastery to plead to be allowed to live as a hermit nearby. The atmosphere of humility and piety in her prayer 'Madre, pietosa Vergina' is sustained throughout the rest of the scene giving an overall sense of reverence and serenity. In complete contrast is the humorous character of Fra Melitone, one of the monks, who certainly prefers the things of the flesh to the things of the spirit and who finds giving charity to the importunate poor extremely irksome. When dismissed by the Father Superior who wishes to talk in private with Leonora he mutters: 'Always secrets! And only these holy ones can know them. We others are so many cabbages.' Mussorgsky's monk Varlaam in *Boris Godounov* (first produced in its entirety in St Petersburg in 1874) owes much to Fra Melitone. This monk and the scenes of camp life were taken from Schiller's *Wallensteins Lager* in a translation by Maffei, and they provide a stark contrast and oblique comment on the gloomy story of outmoded honour and revenge in the rest of the opera.

In a letter of 17 November 1862 Verdi recounted to Contessa Maffei how much they had enjoyed their second visit to Russia: 'In these two months I've been frequenting salons, then there were suppers, parties, etc. I've met both important and humble people, men and women of great amiability and really exquisite *politesse*, quite different from the impertinent Parisian *politesse*.' No doubt one topic of conversation in Russia then was Turgenev's *Fathers and Sons*, which had just been published. This was in fact an important time for literature since the previous three years had seen not only the emergence of Wilkie Collins' *The Woman in White*, George Eliot's *Silas*

Genoa. Engraving by E.J. Roberts (Mary Evans)

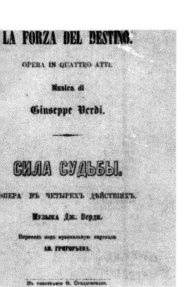

The title page of the
original Russian libretto
of *La forza del destino*, St
Petersburg 1862

Marner and *The Mill on the Floss*, and Victor Hugo's *Les Misérables*, but also Darwin's *Origin of Species*, which was to reverberate throughout the scientific and christian world.

Soon they had to leave for Madrid where the original version of *Forza* was given its Spanish *première* with the aged Duke of Rivas in the audience, after which the Verdis travelled in Andalusia visiting Seville, Cordova, Granada and Cadiz. Verdi bought a cask of sherry to be shipped back to Sant' Agata. From Spain they went directly to Paris where Verdi had agreed to direct a new production of *Vêpres*, but during the hot July weather he clashed with the orchestra over the amount of rehearsal necessary, so returned to his beloved Sant' Agata.

From 1860 Verdi and Giuseppina had begun to spend their winters in Genoa, where eventually Mariani found them part of a *palazzo* to rent, as Giuseppina explained to Clarina Maffei in a letter of 14 June 1867:

The sun, the trees, the flowers and the vast and varied family of the birds, which make country life so lively and beautiful for a great part of the year, leave it sad, mute and bare in the winter. Then I love it no longer. When the snow covers these vast plains round Sant' Agata, and the trees with their bare branches look like desolate skeletons, I can't bear to raise my eyes and look out. I cover the windows with flowered curtains, up to eye-level, and I feel an infinite sadness, a desire to flee from the country, and to feel that I live among the living, and not among the spectres and the silence of a vast cemetery. Verdi, an iron nature, would perhaps have loved the country even in winter and known how to create for himself pleasure and occupations adapted to the season, but he had, in his goodness, compassion on my isolation, and my sadness, and, after many hesitations over the choice of locality, we have pitched our winter tents facing the sea and the mountains, and now I am engaged in furnishing the fifth and certainly the last home of my life.

It was in 1865 that, at Escudier's suggestion, Verdi revised *Macbeth*; but he did not go to Paris for the rehearsals much to Giuseppina's annoyance as she declared she was 'royally bored' at Sant' Agata. The *Macbeth* revival did not go well, partly because it was still basically the work of the thirty-four year old composer, whose audiences expected more of him in 1865.

However, Verdi did agree to write a new work for the Opéra to be performed during the Paris Universal Exhibition of 1867. Once more rejecting *King Lear*, he settled on Schiller's play *Don Carlos*, for which the elderly Joseph Méry was to write the libretto, though it was finished by Camille du Locle on Méry's death. By choosing a subject that contained not only·spectacle

Verdi in 1867, the year when *Don Carlos* was first given at the Paris Opéra

Giuseppina. Oil painting, anonymous

but also interesting character studies, Verdi intended to elevate French Grand Opera in a new way. Neither Schiller's play nor Verdi's opera bears much relation to historical fact, since the historical malformed epileptic Don Carlos, son of Philip II of Spain, becomes a fit young man opposed to his father's tyranny—an antagonism reinforced by his love for, and previous betrothal to, his father's Queen, Elisabetta di Valois. All six principals (the others being the Princess of Eboli, the Marquis of Posa and the Grand Inquisitor) are finely drawn as individual characters and the range of relationships explored surpasses all his other operas. But Verdi and his librettists made two mistakes in changing Schiller's text. They make Carlos fail to recognise that Eboli is not Elisabetta at their secret assignation—which audiences rightly feel to be patently absurd—and they altered the end of the play so that, after Philip has handed over his son to the Grand Inquisitor saying: 'I have done my duty. Now do yours' (the final line of Schiller's play), in the opera a monk, apparently Philip's father (the Emperor Charles V) spirits Don Carlos away from the clutches of the Inquisition.

Verdi's work on *Don Carlos* in the summer of 1866 at Sant' Agata was slowed down by domestic and national problems. A severe bout of his sore throat coupled with anxiety and extreme fatigue made work at times impossible, so much so that he later recalled that without the companionship of Black, the watchdog, he could not have completed the opera. Indeed so much did Verdi feel Black to be involved that he had written a letter as if from him to Arrivabene's dog, Ron-Ron, in August 1865 giving the news that a new opera was under way: 'My male and female secretaries send you their greetings. As regards the first, I read in some paper or other that he's getting ready to make some more little hooks'. (A reference to the fact that Verdi had overheard some peasants on his estate expressing incredulity that he could make a living by putting little hooks on pieces of ruled paper.) Animals held a special part in his and Giuseppina's affections. Both declared that when meeting peasants and livestock in the fields they 'greatly preferred the four-legged variety'. Although Verdi would not allow her to replace Loulou with another pet dog because of her distress at its death, Giuseppina had a parrot (sent by Mariani) and a peacock 'that stands watching me, and tells me that the animals are the best of living beings. That's what my poor Loulou always told me, with his big eyes full of affection and fidelity. Poor Loulou!'

The Battle of Lissa, 20 July 1866 (Mary Evans)

The other interruption to his work on *Don Carlos* was the Austro-Prussian War (The Seven Weeks' War) that began in mid-June 1866. At one time it was thought that Crown Prince Umberto might lodge at Sant' Agata to boost national pride. Like all Italians, Verdi was downcast at the calamitous part Italy played in the war with the defeat of the army at Custoza being followed by the naval disaster at Lissa. In this first naval encounter between steam ironclad ships, seven Austrian vessels defeated fourteen Italian ships, sinking the flagship. When Garibaldi (in whose volunteer ranks were Boito and Faccio) was ordered to withdraw from Trentino, which he had been on the point of taking, the Italian humiliation was complete, although it was some consolation that, Prussia having defeated Austria, Venice was ceded to France and handed over to Italy by Napoleon III. Verdi, who had gone to Paris at the end of July, wrote in disgust to Arrivabene: 'Imagine what it is like to be a patriotic Italian and find oneself in Paris now!' He tried to persuade the Opéra to cancel his contract but they refused.

After he had visited the Pyrenean spa of Cauterets both for his health and to finish the last act of *Don Carlos* 'in peace and

Count Opprandino
Arrivabene (1807–86),
one of Verdi's regular
correspondents

quiet', he returned with Giuseppina to Paris in August. When Verdi received the news that his eighty-two year old father had died, the rehearsals were interrupted not only because he was upset, but also because he was worried about his aunt of eighty-three and her seven year old grand-daughter who were now in the charge of two servants. The little girl was called Filomena, and had lived with Carlo Verdi because her parents were poor peasants with a large family. Verdi and Giuseppina had always taken a great interest in her and were later to adopt her, after which they renamed her Maria. She was sent away to school in Turin and eventually married the son of their friend the lawyer, Dr Angiolo Carrara. Another joy of this period was seeing Muzio again, over from America on a visit with his young wife, Lucy Simons.

On 12 March 1867 Verdi wrote to Count Arrivabene: 'Don Carlos yesterday evening: it wasn't a success!! I don't know what will happen after this, but I shouldn't be surprised if matters were to change.' The *première* was notable for the way in which the Empress Eugénie ostentatiously turned her back on hearing Philip's 'Tais-toi, prêtre' ('Silence, priest') to the Grand Inquisitor. At this first production *Don Carlos* was given only the minimum number of performances stipulated in the contract; yet, in contrast to such a hesitant beginning, there are many today who would consider it to be Verdi's masterpiece. After the Italian *première* at Bologna under Mariani had gone fairly well, Verdi revised parts of it on many occasions. Indeed the history of the score is the most complex of all Verdian operas. For example, at one of the final rehearsals it was discovered that the work was so long that the audience would not be able to catch the last train, so a quarter of an hour had to be cut. The excised material has recently been discovered in orchestral parts where the pages had been stitched together when the cuts were made.

Critics of *Don Carlos* accused Verdi of imitating Wagner. For example, Bizet commented: 'Verdi is no longer Italian; he wants to be like Wagner. He has no longer his own defects; but he also lacks a single one of his qualities.' 'In other words', Verdi retorted in a letter to Escudier on 1 April 1867: 'I'm almost a perfect Wagnerian. But if the critics had paid a little more attention they would have noticed that there are the same kind of ideas present in the *terzetto* from *Ernani*, in the sleepwalking scene from *Macbeth* and in so many other places … But the point is not to know whether *Don Carlos* belongs to this or that system but whether the music is good or bad.'

The charge of being an imitator of Wagner was made many

times in Verdi's lifetime, but it was unjust. At this time he had not even read Wagner's prose works, because in 1869 he wrote asking Camille du Locle to obtain copies for him. He heard the *Tannhäuser* overture at a concert in Paris in 1865, *Lohengrin* in Bologna in 1870 and the whole of *Tannhäuser* in 1875, but probably nothing more. *Die Meistersinger* was first performed the year after *Don Carlos*, as was Brahms' *German Requiem*. Verdi's concern was with tuneful melodies, with music for music's sake, and he once professed himself to be adamantly against all 'schools' and 'isms'. Although his genius continually introduced fresh developments, they were the fruits of experience and not based on theories. When Filippi said of *Aida* that to deny Wagner's influence on the composer would be like denying that the sun gave light, Verdi exclaimed in a

The principal cast of the Bologna production of *Don Carlos*, 1867, including Teresa Stolz and the conductor Angelo Mariani

letter to Ricordi in April 1875: 'A fine result after a career of thirty-five years to end up as an imitator!' The German conductor, Hans von Bülow, long identified with the Wagner camp, attacked Verdi's *Requiem* without having heard it, but in 1892 wrote to Verdi 'the confession of a contrite sinner' for, having studied *Aida*, *Otello* and the *Requiem*, he was 'converted'. Verdi's reply of 14 April 1892 was generous and constructive:

There is no trace of sin in you, and there is no need to talk of repentance and absolution! If your earlier opinions were different from those you profess today, you were very right to make them known; I would never have complained of it. Besides, who knows? … perhaps you were right then? …

If the artists of north and south exhibit different tendencies, it is good that they are different! They should all hold on to the character of their own nation, as Wagner truly says.

In one matter, however, Verdi did follow Wagner. When suggesting to La Scala that the orchestra should be placed in a pit so that they did not interpose between the audience and the action, he said: 'The idea is not mine, but Wagner's, and it is excellent.'

After *Don Carlos*, life in the country once more proved a haven to Verdi. When he was in a bad mood the peasants escaped from him by finding work in the farthest fields. Undoubtedly he ran his farms well but could be a tyrannical overseer, refusing to let the men use the machinery when he wasn't there and demanding to know why on earth his foreman, Paolo Marenghi, had spent so much money in his absence. Giuseppina, lonely in the house, would scarcely get a word out of him all day. So it isn't surprising that, while on a shopping expedition to Milan, she decided to call to see Clarina Maffei, whom she had never met. Their immediate liking for each other led the Contessa to take her to see the eighty-two year old novelist and poet, Alessandro Manzoni, who gave her a photograph of himself to take to her husband inscribed: 'To Giuseppe Verdi, a glory of Italy, from a decrepit Lombard writer.' Verdi revered the author of *I promessi sposi* (*The Betrothed*), a novel he described as 'not only the greatest book of our age, but one of the greatest books ever to have come out of the human mind. It isn't only a book, it's a consolation for humanity'. He was therefore overwhelmed at the thought of meeting Manzoni, which he did a year later. 'How can I describe to you', he wrote to Clarina on 7 July 1868 'the new, the sweet, the indefinable sensation I experienced in the presence of the Saint, as you call him? If mortal men could be adored I would have knelt before him.' Verdi was also delighted that Clarina paid them a visit to Sant' Agata and he sent her away laden with 'whole forests of flowers'.

Before that meeting took place two sad events added to Verdi's gloom and despondency. On 21 July 1867 Antonio Barezzi died. The Verdis were with him at the end. He lay quietly in bed and then looked with longing at the piano in the corner of the room. Verdi went over to it and began to play softly Signor Antonio's favourite piece—'Va, pensiero' the chorus of captive Jews from *Nabucco*. The old man raised a hand, murmured 'Oh, my Verdi', and died peacefully. To

Installing an exhibit in the British section of the 1867 Paris Exhibition (Mary Evans)

Clarina Maffei Verdi wrote: 'You know that I owe him everything, everything, everything.'

After this loss the Verdis went with Mariani to see the Exhibition in Paris. The brilliance of the Empire was beginning to fade, but this Exhibition of 1867 filled the French capital once more with the crowned heads of Europe who came to wonder at the miracles of science on display: the marvellous new lightweight metal aluminium; the recent American invention of the rocking-chair; and of course the new steam locomotives. An unnoticed shadow from the future was cast when Krupp of Essen won a prize with a great gun; but on a lighter note missionary societies showed off their trophies of heathen weapons to a public amused by such novelties. Yet it was the city's new sewerage system that attracted most interest for the small boats and cars that were designed to traverse the subterranean routes in order to clean them could, on occasion, take visitors. These sight-seeing tours during the Exhibition were so successful that they have continued until the present day. Verdi much admired the new Opéra building designed by Garnier. Work had been going on for six years behind high wooden screens and it was not to be opened until 1874, but in the year of the Exhibition the screens

The new Paris Opéra
(Mary Evans)

were removed to reveal the main front, which many condemned as looking like 'a cluttered sideboard'.

However such pleasant excursions were halted by another piece of sad news. Piave had a stroke and was paralysed, unable to move or speak during the eight years he lingered on. His wife advised against a visit, but Verdi helped them financially and organised an *Album* of songs by various composers for Piave's benefit.

To sadness was now added irritation. Since 1845 the citizens of Busseto had wanted to build a small opera house. At various stages it was suggested that Verdi would write an opera for the opening-night; or that he would persuade some leading singers to come; or that he would contribute a large part of the cost. Verdi repeatedly stated that he thought these demands ridiculous. Giuseppina kept a kind of dossier on the transactions over the years and it seems quite clear that she encouraged her husband's intransigent attitude; but after all she did have many bitter memories of her treatment in the past. In the end, Verdi allowed his name to be given to the theatre, and he 'contributed' by writing off a loan of 10,000 lire he had made to the town for the re-building of a bridge. But he did not attend the opening night on 15 August 1868 when, before a performance of *Rigoletto,* an overture he was supposed to have written at the age of twelve was followed by the curtain rising to reveal a bust of him crowned by a wreath of flowers. He would have loathed it. Later, having received a nasty anonymous letter, he sold his box in the theatre. The tiny theatre which holds just over a hundred still exists but, although Toscanini once staged *Aida* there, it is so small that festival performances are usually given in the *piazza* in front of it.

Verdi's creative genius remained unclouded by such personal difficulties, even though this did seem to be a time in his life when 'the force of destiny' was working inexorably to remove many whom he had valued and loved.

The Teatro Verdi,
Busseto, opened in 1868

Chapter 8
Public Glory And Private Sorrow

'Dear, dear friend! That man was a prodigious, artist! A genius! A genius of music and the theatre!'—Boito

Death now removed another link with the past. Rossini died in Paris on 13 November 1868. Feeling the loss not only for himself as a friend, but for Italy and for music, Verdi wrote a public letter four days later to Tito Ricordi in the Milan *Gazzetta Musicale*:

> To honour the memory of Rossini, I should like to ask the most distinguished Italian composers (Mercadante above all, if only with a few bars) to compose a Requiem Mass to be performed on the anniversary of his death. I should like not only the composers but also the performers to give their services free and also contribute a small amount towards the expenses.
>
> The Mass should be performed in the church of San Petronio in the city of Bologna, which was Rossini's real musical home. This Mass should be an object neither of curiosity nor of speculation. After the performance, it should be sealed, and placed in the archives of the Music Academy of that city, whence it should never be removed. Perhaps an exception could be made for future anniversaries of his death, should posterity wish to celebrate them.

While this project was under way, he directed rehearsals of a revised *La forza del destino* which was enthusiastically received at La Scala, Milan, on 27 February 1869, marking not only the healing of his relations with Italy's premier opera house, but also the beginning of his connection with the soprano Teresa Stolz. Meanwhile owing to the lack of co-operation by Scalaberni, impresario of the Bologna theatre, a suitable chorus could not be found to sing the Requiem Mass for Rossini. Verdi wrote on 19 November to Clarina Maffei: 'The Bologna affair is an ugly business for many people, including my distinguished friend Mariani, who has not lifted a finger in this affair which I so recommended to him. The Milanese committee, in my opinion, can do only one thing: restore the pieces to their respective composers and say no more about it.' This is what happened.

Angelo Mariani (1821–73). Apart from being a supporter of Verdi, he also championed Wagner, introducing *Lohengrin* to Italian audiences in 1871

The banks of the Po near
Sant' Agata

Verdi was bitterly disappointed, but was unjust to blame
Mariani who had been one of his closest friends. It was he who
had found the Verdis the apartment in the Palazzo Sauli in
Genoa for their winter retreat 'situated on the hill of
Carignano, amid gardens with cypresses, cedars, palms and
magnolias, with wide views over the port and the shining sea'.
Mariani had a 'nest' there and on many occasions
accompanied the Verdis to Paris and elsewhere. He and Verdi
shared a passion for shooting woodcock, pheasant and the like
in the woods near the River Po. He gladly undertook
commissions for Verdi, one of which involved him in
transporting ten magnolias a metre-and-a-half high to Sant'
Agata from Genoa even though they would not fit into the
luggage van of the train! Yet now, although he does not seem
to have been in the least to blame for the failure of the Rossini
project, Verdi placed him in the wrong. Mariani became like a
cringing spaniel trying to ingratiate itself with a displeased
master. His letters to Verdi at this time all end with some
phrase like: 'Forgive me, my Maestro, if I annoy you with
these stupid letters of mine.'

However the production of *Don Carlos* in Paris had led the
Verdis to a new and affectionate friendship with the du Locles,
a friendship that lasted till death, in spite of one catastrophe
that caused a break in the friendship for some time. In the late
1860s Camille du Locle bombarded his new composer friend
with suggestions for libretti, including, surprisingly, many

119

comedies amongst which was Molière's *Tartuffe*. This was fairly courageous of du Locle for in December 1869 he received a long diatribe against the Opéra from Verdi:

Everyone wants to give an opinion or express doubt; and, if a composer lives too long in this atmosphere of doubt, he cannot escape having his convictions shaken a little, and begins to correct and adjust, or, to put it better, to look askance at his own work. Thus, in the end, you have not a work in one piece, but a mosaic. That may be fine, if you like it, but it's still a mosaic. You may reply that the Opéra has produced a string of masterpieces in this manner. They may be masterpieces, but allow me to say that they would be even more perfect if this pieced-together feeling and these adjustments were not so obvious at every point. No one, surely, will deny the genius of Rossini. All right, but, despite all his genius, his *Guillaume Tell* has about it this fatal atmosphere of the Opéra ... The conclusion of all this is that I am not a composer for Paris. I don't know whether I have any talent or not, but I know for certain that my ideas of art are quite different from yours.

During a brief visit to Paris at the end of March 1870 Verdi was favourably impressed with the Opéra-Comique where du Locle had recently taken over as manager. He also saw Emanuele Muzio again who had just returned from Cairo where he had been directing the first season of the new Viceregal opera house opened in November 1869 at about the same time as the Suez Canal.

The Director of the new Cairo Opera House, Draneht Bey, had asked Verdi to compose an ode for its opening; but, disliking such *morceaux de circonstance*, the composer had refused.

The Canal, linking the Mediterranean and the Red Sea across a hundred miles of sand from Port Said to Suez, had been the vision of a Frenchman, Ferdinand de Lesseps. Against apparently insuperable odds he had carried out the work in ten years. At the start he had had only native Egyptian workmen (the *fellahin*) to dig out the sand by hand and only baskets on camels to transport it away; but later enormous mechanical dredgers had been used. On 16 November 1868 the Canal had been opened by an enormous flotilla led by the side-paddle yacht *L'Aigle* with the French Empress Eugénie and de Lesseps on board. Many other European royalty were also there, including Emperor Franz Josef of Austro-Hungary. Half-way down the new waterway the guests spent the night at the new town of Ismailia where they were entertained by the Khedive of Egypt, Ismail Pasha, in a fairy-tale setting of ornate palaces decorated with flowers and lights, red-cloaked

The opening of the Suez Canal: the Empress Eugénie of France and Ferdinand de Lesseps on board the *Aigle* entering the canal at Port Said, 16 November 1869.
Illustrated London News (Mary Evans)

Bedouin guards on white camels, Egyptian cavalry on magnificent horses, a picnic in the desert with a display by thirty thousand Arabs, and fireworks illuminating the night sky before the opening journey down the Canal was completed the next day.

The Cairo Opera opened with a performance of *Rigoletto*, after which du Locle informed Verdi that the Khedive still hoped that he would write a new opera for Cairo, even though offers of increasingly good terms failed to tempt him. However, at the end of May, when Verdi asked du Locle for a synopsis of a Spanish play, the crafty Parisian also sent him four pages outlining a story by the Egyptologist Auguste Mariette. He had been sent by the French Government in 1850 to purchase ancient manuscripts in Egypt, where he had eventually settled, become an archaeologist, and made some of the most important nineteenth century discoveries of Egyptian treasures, including the tombs of the Pharaohs at Abydos, Giza and elsewhere. He had been appointed Curator of Ancient Monuments and honoured with the title 'Bey' by the Khedive. We shall probably never know whether Verdi was won over by Mariette's subject, or by the postscript to his letter, which instructed du Locle that 'if M. Verdi does not accept, His Highness begs you to knock at another door ... Gounod and even Wagner are being considered. The latter, if he would be willing, could do something really grand'. At any rate Verdi immediately responded on 26 May:

I have read the Egyptian programme. It is well made; the *mise-en-scène* is splendid, and there are one or two situations which if not entirely new are certainly very fine. But who wrote it? Behind it all is the hand of an expert ... thoroughly familiar with the stage.

The origins of *Aida* remained the subject of dispute for many years. Verdi later claimed that, though he had been told that the Khedive himself was the author, he did not believe it. There seems little doubt that it was actually written by Mariette Bey, and that du Locle then expanded it by incorporating ideas from other sources. For example, the story has many points of contact with the plots of *Nitteti* (by the eighteenth century librettist Metastasio) and Racine's *Bajazet*. Verdi was therefore absolutely correct to call this subject 'not entirely new'. One reflects on what might have happened if Verdi had attempted to set some of the works of Ibsen or Dostoyevsky, or even Tolstoy's *War and Peace*, which all appeared in the late 1860s.

The Cairo contract provided that Verdi was to be paid four times the amount he had received for *Don Carlos*, which prompted him to stipulate: 'The figure must remain secret, for otherwise it would be a pretext to trouble so many of the unfortunate departed. They would not fail to quote the four hundred crowns paid for *Il barbiere di Siviglia*, the poverty of Beethoven, the misery of Schubert, the vagabondage of Mozart to make a living, etc., etc.' Mariette gained a trip to Paris for himself and his family at the Viceroy's expense as 'professional consultant', but du Locle, although he paid a visit to Sant' Agata to draw up the prose libretto with Verdi, was not involved further. Instead, Antonio Ghislanzoni was summoned to the Villa Verdi with the offer of a generous fee. Hearing of the ferocity of the three mastiffs at Sant' Agata, he threatened to arrive with a Nubian slave 'to throw as dogs' meat', so as to protect his own legs. Ghislanzoni's previous career somewhat recalls the diversity of Temistocle Solera, for, starting out as a medical student, he had been in turn a double bass player, baritone, journalist, novelist and playwright. Because he cared little for convention, his behaviour was often eccentric. He once caused considerable consternation in Milan by striding through the cathedral square in the uniform of an ancient Roman general, having forgotten to change after an opera performance.

Teresa Stolz (1834–1902) in the rôle of Aida at La Scala, 1872

Antonio Ghislanzoni
(1824–93), the librettist of
Aida and editor of the
Gazzetta musicale in Milan

Although Verdi had asked for plenty of time to compose the opera 'since we're dealing with a work of truly vast proportions, as it might be for the *Grande Boutique*' (his term of abuse for the Paris Opéra), in the event he composed the music as fast as Ghislanzoni wrote the verses. By mid-November, in only four months, *Aida* was all but complete. Unlike his treatment of poor Piave, Verdi was fairly courteous to Ghislanzoni, who was recognized as Italy's leading librettist of the time. Nevertheless there was the usual intense collaboration over the shaping of the text with Verdi expressing his own views firmly. It is surprising to learn that Verdi himself wrote the famous tenor *cavatina* 'Celeste Aida' as a '*romanze* to be added at the singer's pleasure'. In his consultations with Ghislanzoni, Verdi at one moment proposed conventional ideas like this, while at another he was prepared to abandon formal verses 'so as to be able to say clearly and precisely everything the action demands. Unfortunately, for the theatre it is sometimes necessary that poets and composers have the talent to make neither poetry nor music.' Yet *Aida* remains a perfection of musical structure within the Rossinian model, contrasting with the 'questing' *Don Carlos* that preceded it : it is, to use Julian Budden's parallel, the 'faultless classical symmetry' of a *Così fan tutte* following the prophetic *Don Giovanni*.

The setting of *Aida* is 'the time of the Pharaohs'. Radames is given command of the Egyptian army to fight against the invading Ethiopians. Such high politics are governed, however, by an eternal triangle. The Pharaoh's daughter Amneris loves Radames, but she discovers by a trick that he is in love with her Ethiopian slave Aida. When the Egyptians return victorious, Radames is promised the hand of Amneris as reward. One of his captives turns out to be Aida's father, Amonasro. He makes Aida find out from Radames at their secret lovers' meeting the route the Egyptian army is to take when attacking Ethiopia. Discovering with horror that he has been overheard by Amonasro, now revealed as King of Ethiopia, Radames is condemned to death by entombment for his treachery. In the magnificent final scene the stage is split into two levels : above is the Temple where Amneris prays for peace and the priestesses praise mighty Phtha, while on the lower level in the sealed tomb Radames and Aida, who has crept in to join him, die in each other's arms.

Verdi spent some time finding out about ancient Egyptian customs and instruments, but ended up by inventing his own brand of Egyptian music that sounds plausible and brings

The final scene of *Aida* in the Paris production of 1880. *L'Illustration* (Mary Evans)

exotic colour to the opera. Meanwhile Mariette had supervised the creation of authentic costumes and sets in Paris for the Cairo *première*, but he and his family were to find their 'holiday' in the French capital extended throughout the next cold winter by *force majeure*. On 19 July 1870 the Franco-Prussian War began with everyone expecting Napoleon III to dispose speedily of Bismarck. Quite the reverse happened. On 2 September the Prussians defeated the French at the Battle of Sedan and took Napoleon and most of his army prisoner. A bloodless revolution took place on 4 September in Paris, the Empress Eugénie slipped away to England, and yet another French Republic was created. However a fortnight later the Prussian army laid siege to the city and, since the only escape and means of communication was by balloon or pigeon post, Mariette, along with the costumes and scenery for *Aida*, was trapped with the rest of the population of Paris. An anonymous commentator wrote in the New Year of 1871:

The sufferings of Paris were a joke for two months. In the third month the joke went sour. Now nobody finds it funny any more, and we are moving fast towards starvation or, for the moment at least, towards an epidemic of gastritis. Half a pound of horsemeat, including the bones, which is two people's rations for three days, is lunch for an ordinary appetite. The prices of edible chicken or pies put them out of reach. Failing meat, you cannot fall back on vegetables: a little turnip costs eight sous, and you have to pay seven francs for a pound of onions. Nobody talks about butter any more, and every other sort of fat except candle-fat and axle-grease has disappeared too. As for the two staple items of the diet of the poorer classes—potatoes and cheese—cheese is just a memory and you have to have friends in high places to obtain potatoes at twenty francs a bushel. The greater part of Paris is living on coffee, wine and bread.

The food shortage was somewhat alleviated by the killing of animals in the zoo, including the two elephants; dogs, cats and rats were mercilessly hunted, with men crouched in the gutters by the sewer gulleys hoping to catch an emerging rat.

Verdi had never intended to attend the Cairo presentation of *Aida*, but he had set great store by the Italian first-night due a month later at La Scala. Admitting that the siege of Paris should be considered an 'act of God', he agreed to postpone the Italian performance until the Cairo *première* could be given.

Dogs, cats and rats for sale during the Siege of Paris, 1870–71. Illustration from H. Vizetelley's *Paris in Peril*, Vol. II (London 1882)

The Paris Commune, 1871: barricades of paving stones manned, ironically, in the Rue de la Paix. A photograph (Mary Evans)

Because the French had withdrawn from Rome, Vittorio Emanuele was able to send Italian troops to occupy the 'Patrimony of St Peter', forcing Pope Pio Nono to withdraw into the Vatican thereby bringing about the demise of the Papal States. But this important day for Italian unity was overshadowed by the events in France for most Italians including Verdi. He declared that 'the business at Rome is a great event but it leaves me cold', while 'this disaster for France desolates my heart ... after all France gave liberty and civilization to the modern world. If she falls, let us not deceive ourselves all our liberty and civilization will fall too.' He asked du Locle to set aside two thousand francs of his advance for *Aida* to help the French wounded.

At this moment he was offered a most important appointment, that of Director of the Naples Conservatory, in succession to Mercadante who had died on 17 December. Acknowledging the honour with gratitude, Verdi declined. He was no academic and valued his freedom. He was eventually persuaded, however, to preside over a government commission to recommend reforms for Italy's Conservatories. His rallying cry was 'Let us turn to the past: that will be progress' for, like so many whose education has been successful, he thought that a repetition of the recipe was the answer for the next generation.

Paris capitulated in January after the Prussians began to shell the city and King William had been proclaimed first German Emperor in the Hall of Mirrors at Versailles. The new French Assembly of the Third Republic was republican only in name. Garibaldi and Victor Hugo were both shouted down when they tried to address it and both left the country in disgust. When the Assembly moved to Versailles and began to temporise with the Germans, revolutionary elements set up the 'Commune' of Paris ('commune' being the medieval term for a chartered city). The second siege of Paris now began as French troops surrounded the city under the eyes of the silent German army. The 'Communards', having shot sixty-seven hostages including the Archbishop of Paris and having burnt down the palace of the Tuileries, the Hôtel de Ville and the Palais de Justice, were themselves massacred by the troops storming into the city four days later. Between twenty and thirty thousand people were shot, including many women and children, and thousands more were deported to New Caledonia. A shocked Verdi wrote to Luccardi: 'Events in France are painful and astounding. Principles pushed to extremes lead only to disorder. France, or rather, Paris, pushed both good and evil to extremes, and these are the results.' At last the Mariette family plus the scenery and costumes were released so that the Cairo *première* of *Aida* could be arranged.

The critic of *La Perseveranza*, Filippo Filippi, wrote to Verdi to let him know that he would be attending the *première* of *Aida* in Cairo. The rôle of music critics changed considerably during the course of the nineteenth century: previously their job had been simply that of reporter, recording the judgement of the audience, but gradually men like Filippi gave their own critique of works and assumed an authority to which many musicians felt they had no claim. Verdi found critics a mixed blessing and responded to Filippi's offer to do anything he could for him in Cairo by a letter of 8 December 1871:

Filippo Filippi (1830–87), the music critic of *La Perseveranza*. A caricature by Cima

I always remember joyfully my first years when, almost without a single friend, without anyone to talk to me, without preparations, without any kind of influence being exerted on my behalf, I presented my operas to the public, ready to exchange shots, and extremely happy if I managed to make an occasional favourable impression. Nowadays, what an apparatus accompanies each opera! Journalists, soloists, chorus, conductors, players etc. etc., all must carry their stone to the edifice of publicity, to build up a framework of wretched gossip which adds nothing to the merit of an opera, but merely obscures its real value. This is deplorable, deeply deplorable!!

In the event, the first performances of *Aida* in Cairo on Christmas Eve 1871 and in Milan on 8 February 1872 were both a great success. Verdi wrote to Count Opprandino Arrivabene the day after the Milan first night: 'The audience liked it. I don't want to play at being modest with you: this is

The first performance of *Aida*, Cairo, 24 December 1871 (Mary Evans)

by no means the worst thing I've written, and time will give it the place it deserves. In short, it's a success and will pack the theatre.' Nevertheless some critics once more accused him of 'Wagnerisms' to his considerable annoyance, while a certain Prospero Bertani, who had twice travelled from Reggio to Parma to see the opera, disliked the music so much that the money he had wasted preyed 'like a spectre' on his mind, so he sent Verdi a bill for two train journeys, theatre tickets and 'a detestable supper at the station'. Verdi good-humouredly instructed Ricordi to pay him, less the amount for the suppers since 'he could perfectly well have eaten at home. Naturally he must send you a receipt, as well as a written undertaking not to attend another new opera of mine, so that he won't expose himself again to the danger of being pursued by spectres or involve me in further travel expenses.'

The Aida for the performances at La Scala was Teresa Stolz, a Bohemian by birth. Her twin sisters achieved considerable notoriety when they both lived with the composer Luigi Ricci, visiting him from their adjoining lodgings through a concealed door in a wardrobe, although they occasionally mistimed their entrances and emerged from the wardrobe while Ricci was entertaining 'respectable' visitors. Teresa,

A page from Wagner's *Lohengrin*, annotated by Verdi on the occasion of the opera's first Italian performance, in Bologna in 1871 under the direction of Mariani

born in 1834, studied at Prague Conservatory and soon started on a highly successful career as an operatic soprano. She eventually became engaged to the conductor Angelo Mariani. Verdi's growing interest in the soprano may well have been a factor in the **deterioration of** the friendship between the conductor and composer. Certainly the Verdis encouraged the soprano to break off her relationship with Mariani in the autumn of 1871, after she had been to stay at Sant' Agata. The conductor wrote bitterly to a friend: 'She is now very intimate with Verdi, which proves what affection she had for me!! Who would have ever thought that my friends, the two persons I esteemed and loved more than myself, would have united in treating me as they have done !!!!! ' In fact Verdi had to press Mariani hard to return some of Stolz's savings which he had borrowed and not paid back.

When the publisher Francesco Lucca, as another stage in his war with Verdi's publisher Ricordi, commissioned Mariani to conduct a performance of *Lohengrin* at Bologna in 1871, Verdi travelled to Bologna to hear Wagner's opera, but rudely

Teresa Stolz. A painting

Giuseppina in 1878

rebuffed Mariani who, having met him by accident on the station, offered to carry his bag. The Maestro's presence seems to have put everyone off and the performance was a poor one, causing Verdi to scribble many derogatory notes in the margin of his score.

Mariani was bitterly wounded by Verdi's treatment of him, and by the fact that next autumn, while he was conducting a production of *Tannhäuser* at Bologna, the Verdis were much seen with Teresa Stolz in Naples where they had gone for productions of *Don Carlos* and *Aida*. Mariani was gravely ill with cancer and, alone in his rooms in Verdi's house in Genoa, he died later that year ravaged by pain and constant haemorrhages. 'What a loss for Art' was Verdi's only recorded reaction to the death of one who had once been such a dear friend.

It is impossible to say whether or not Verdi and Stolz were lovers, but there is no doubt that he was extremely attracted by her. Giuseppina's unhappiness at this time is plainly evident from her letters; there were rows at Sant' Agata; Verdi seemed to take more than a usual interest in the soprano's affairs, while she herself wrote both the Verdis so many letters that Giuseppina once commented sharply: 'Sixteen letters!! In so short a time!! What activity!' In fact the letters that survive are fairly innocuous, dealing with her visits to see them, or with theatrical gossip. Yet Giuseppina's black mood intensified, as she revealed in her letters to friends. Typical is one to Clarina Maffei on 15 March 1874:

Having arrived at a certain age, one lives much on memories. We all have them, happy, sorrowful and dear, but alas! we are not all so fortunate as to conserve unchanged the affection and the friendship of the living, or at least the illusion of possessing those things, which make life dear.

In September 1875 the *Rivista Indipendente* of Florence published a scurrilous attack on Verdi and Stolz in which it was alleged, amongst other things, that Verdi's wallet had slipped out of his pocket onto the sofa in Teresa's Milan hotel room while the couple were engaged in amorous pursuits, and that the wallet was later found there by a waiter much to the singer's confusion. Yet Giuseppina immediately assured her that she would still be welcome at the Villa Verdi. It must be said that neither seemed to seek occasion to be *à deux* with the other: once Stolz brought Maria Waldmann with her when she was invited alone; for his part Verdi refused to go to Russia to conduct a performance in which Stolz was singing. Furthermore in their letters they never used the intimate form

Verdi in 1873.
Terracotta bust by V.
Gemito (Villa Verdi di
Sant' Agata)

Alessandro Manzoni
(1785–1873) in the last
year of his life. Admired
by Goethe, his most
famous work, *I promessi
sposi* (a romance set in
16th century Milan) was
begun in 1825. Within
fifty years it had run into
118 editions

of address but always the formal second person plural *voi* or
even the third person singular *lei*.

However in April 1876 Giuseppina wrote this draft of a
letter in her book, although it is not known whether Verdi
ever received it:

'It didn't seem to me a fitting day for you to pay a call on a lady
who is neither your daughter, nor your sister, nor your wife!' The
observation escaped me and I perceived at once that you were
annoyed ... it seems to me you could spend twenty-four hours
without seeing the said lady ...

I don't know if there's anything in it, or not ... I do know that
since 1872 there have been periods of assiduity and attentions on
your part that no woman could interpret in a more favourable sense
... If there's anything in it ... Let's get this over. Be frank and say so,
without making me suffer the humiliation of this excessive deference
of yours.

If there's nothing in it ... Be more calm in your attentions, be
natural and less exclusive. Think sometimes that I, your wife,
despising past rumours, am living at this very moment *à trois*, and
that I have the right to ask, if not for your caresses, at least for your
consideration. Is that too much?

Six months later in October, after Teresa Stolz had stayed at
Sant' Agata for some time, Giuseppina drafted another letter
beginning: 'Since fate has willed that that which was my whole
happiness should now be irreparably lost ... ' There is some
evidence that she had even gone to stay with her sister at
Cremona when she wrote this. But the sixty-two year old
Verdi appears to have got over his infatuation (if that is what it
was) for the singer who was after all twenty years his junior,
the tension gradually relaxed, and they all remained good
friends for life. Teresa Stolz continued to visit them on
birthdays and name-days, and sometimes went with them to
Montecatini to take the waters.

During this period of personal drama Verdi had not been
professionally inactive. In the course of their stay in Naples in
early 1873 Stolz fell ill so that the production of *Aida* had to be
postponed. The composer spent the time writing the E minor
String Quartet, which was then performed to a group of
friends in the hotel. Verdi then laid it aside as 'of no
importance', although he was persuaded to publish it in 1877.
He always maintained that it was written for 'mere
amusement' but it is a melodic, even humorous, work, which
if not taken too seriously is quite delightful.

It was followed by another non-operatic work of
considerably more importance. On 22 May 1873 the eighty-
nine year old Manzoni died in Milan. Verdi was too moved to

The first La Scala performance of the *Requiem,* with Maini, Capponi, Waldmann and Stolz under the direction of Verdi himself. In one of her many letters to her confessor, Salvatore Magnasco (the Archbishop of Genoa), Giuseppina left some comments on Verdi's attitude towards religion which are worth recalling: 'Verdi', she wrote, 'is not communicative and expansive but his soul is very sensitive … He is respectful towards religion, is a believer like me and never fails to carry out those practices necessary for a good Christian, such as he wishes to be … Verdi is a good Christian, better than many others who wish to seem so more than he.' In connection with the *Requiem* she argued elsewhere that 'a

attend the funeral of this great Italian he so revered, but he visited the grave alone later. He wrote to Contessa Maffei at the end of May:

With him ends the most pure, the most sacred, the highest of our glories. I have read many of the newspapers, and not one of them speaks of him as he should be spoken of. Many words, but none of them profoundly felt. No lack of stinging remarks, however. Even at him! … Oh, what an ugly race we are!

So, deciding that he would try to write something himself more worthy of the author of *I promessi sposi,* Verdi suggested to the Mayor and Council of Milan that he would compose and pay for the publication of a *Requiem* if they would bear the cost of the first performance. They agreed, so Verdi began work on it during the summer when he was with Giuseppina in Paris, where the Third Republic was uneasily beginning its existence. He was able to use material from the *Libera me* he had written for the ill-fated Rossini *Mass.* The first performance in the Church of San Marco, Milan on 22 May 1874 (the exact anniversary of Manzoni's death) was such a triumphant success that three more performances had to be given at La Scala. The soprano was Teresa Stolz to whom Verdi later gave the manuscript score. It is certainly a work for performance rather than for singing as part of a Mass in Church. It is the work of an operatic composer offering his best. The German pianist and conductor Hans von Bülow, put an announcement in the papers: 'Hans von Bülow was not present at the show yesterday at the Church of San Marco', but Brahms later examined the score and declared: 'Bülow has made a fool of himself. This is a work of genius.' It has already been noted that Bülow later recanted his rash statement.

Continued from previous page
man like Verdi must write like Verdi ... the religious spirit and the way in which it finds expression must bear the imprint of its time and the individuality of the author. I should, so to speak, have repudiated a Mass by Verdi, if it had been modelled on those of A, B or C.'

The *Requiem* was taken on tour and performed in Paris that year and the next, as well as in Vienna and London, where it was given three times at the Albert Hall with a chorus of twelve hundred which contrasted markedly with the hand-picked choir of one hundred and twenty chosen for the San Marco performance. While in England Verdi managed to go to the great Handel Festival at the Crystal Palace. Much of the music of the *Requiem* is vivid and dramatic, especially the setting of the medieval Latin sequence *Dies irae*; but it is also sincere, although the agnostic Verdi offers no final hope since the work ends with the continued uncertainty of the soprano's repeated plea for release from final judgment. Giuseppina commented on the views of those who held that the music was not 'sacred': 'I say that a man like Verdi must write like Verdi, that is according to his own way of feeling and interpreting the text.' Verdi's *Requiem* restates his view that death is all there is in life—an essentially tragic conception of humanity that he was to explore yet again.

The off-stage band in *Aida* during the 1880 Paris production. *L'Illustration*, 30 October 1880 (Mary Evans)

Chapter 9
Two Masterpieces

'The most bewildering aspect of Verdi's genius remains that
unending capacity to take in fresh experience and in each successive
work present something new yet deeply rooted in the past'—Julian
Budden

After *Aida* Verdi seems once again to have given up all
thoughts of further operatic compostion. Fifteen years were to
pass before *Otello* was given its *première*, although he did revise
two operas during this time. In March 1875, however, he
declared to Clarina that the score was settled and that he had
no obligation to anyone to compose more, while in a letter to
Maria Waldmann, written in July 1876 as she was about to
retire from the stage in order to marry, he betrayed a note of
finality, a certain *tristesse* at the end of an era of creativity:

> You have been in Venice for several days now, calm and happy,
> occupied only with rehearsals for the opera this season, which will be
> the last one for you .... The last! It's a sad word which calls up a
> world of memories and embraces a life of excitements, some happy,
> some sad, but always dear to those with the fibres of an artist. You,
> however, are fortunate in that you will find great consolation in your
> change of fortune. It's not so for others, to whom the word 'last'
> means 'Everything is over!'

He went abroad several times in the 1870s for performances
of the *Requiem* as well as in Paris in March 1880 to conduct the
first production in French of *Aida*, but nevertheless his mood
was generally one of despondency and dejection. Of course,
the *ménage à trois* was still causing Giuseppina to grieve during
this arid period in their marriage, yet Verdi himself was
dispirited because of more public matters. He wrote
continually about the rising tide of Germany, the 'heartless,
iron nation' as he called it, that seemed about to engulf the
Italian theatrical tradition, so that, for example, when the
Théâtre des Italiens in Paris closed, putting its conductor
Muzio out of a job, no one felt able to reopen it. In addition,
like so many of his fellow-countrymen, Verdi was disillusioned
because the high hopes of the Risorgimento had not been
realised in practice by the new Kingdom of Italy.

Maria Carrara-Verdi, the composer's adopted daughter

Alberto Carrara

His black mood was further increased when he discovered 'irregularities' in Ricordi's accounts, so, becoming more and more furious, he went through all the contracts relating to the hire of his operas from *Rigoletto* onwards, settling eventually for a payment of fifty-thousand lire in previously unpaid commissions. 'It is less than what is due to me', he wrote and recognised that his relationship with Tito Ricordi could never be the same again. Fortunately the latter's son, Giulio, now took over all dealings with the composer and it is a tribute to his tact and business sense that, not only did he become a valued friend in a way that his father and grandfather had never been, but he was also able to win the Maestro back to composition and his most successful collaboration with a librettist.

The years between *Aida* and *Otello* were soured by dealings with friends in financial difficulties. After the failure of Bizet's *Carmen*, the Opéra Comique collapsed, so Verdi engaged in an unpleasant lawsuit over money he had advanced to du Locle, the theatre's director. Then Escudier failed at the Théâtre des Italiens and Verdi's letters to him thereafter were curt and wounding. Next it was the turn of his Neapolitan friend Cesare de Sanctis who was unable to repay a loan of twenty-five thousand lire. Verdi suggested that it should be paid off in regular consignments of Neapolitan pasta, but he never wrote to de Sanctis again, although the kindly Giuseppina did. Finally, the bailiff at Sant' Agata, Mauro Corticelli, with whom Peppina was very friendly, was discovered to have speculated with, and lost, the savings of two of the servants. When he was sacked, he tried unsuccessfully to commit suicide.

Death continued inexorably to remove many whom Verdi respected or loved. In 1878 King Vittorio Emanuele, Pope Pio Nono, Solera and Piave all died. Although he had not seen the two librettists for some years, and neither the King nor the Pope had gained popular acclaim for their achievements, these deaths marked the passing of an age and heralded years to come in which Verdi would witness the deaths of many he held most dear.

However the same year did bring a happy occasion in the marriage of the nineteen year old Maria Verdi to Alberto Carrara, the son of their friend and lawyer in Busseto. The wedding took place in the recently completed chapel in the Villa Verdi. The families were delighted and when, next year, she had a baby, Verdi proudly wrote: 'You know our Maria has a beautiful baby? I can't describe the joy of everyone,

Giulio Ricordi
(1840–1912). A
photograph

especially of Peppina and the Carrara family. I pray only that this little baby girl will not some day be suffocated ... by kisses.' He and Peppina had moved their winter lodgings in Genoa to twelve rooms in another Palazzo with a suberb view of the harbour, a lovely garden and an enormous terrace, to which they continued to go each winter. Verdi took little part in public life, though in 1875 he was made a Senator of the Kingdom of Italy. Many were dismayed that the official announcement stressed his enormous contribution to Italy in taxes rather than through his music.

It was not until 1879 that Giulio Ricordi's efforts to interest Verdi in an opera once more began to bear fruit. He had already suggested a text by Arrigo Boito, but their previous collaboration on the *Inno delle Nazioni* had been marred by Boito's poem that greeted his friend Franco Faccio's opera *I profughi fiamminghi* (*The Flemish fugitives*) by hailing its composer as the one destined to cleanse the altar of Italian opera 'defiled like the walls of a brothel'. Verdi had written in reply: 'If I too, among others, have soiled the altar, as Boito says, let him clean it and I shall be the first to come and light a candle.' But in fact Boito was a theorist who was unable to put into practice what he taught. He prophesied a new dawn for Italian music, but his opera *Mefistofele*, first produced in 1868, was a disaster, though the revised version of 1875 had some success. He and Verdi were united in 1868 when Emilio Broglio, the Minister of Education, condemned *Don Carlos* (amongst others) and Boito's opera under the labels of respectively 'musical mastodons' and 'Mephistophelian presumptions'. Verdi promptly returned his decoration of the Order of the Crown of Italy, recently awarded to him, with the comment that it must have been sent to the wrong address. Boito for his part wrote a splendid and humorous open letter assuring the Minister that many important operas *had* been composed since Rossini's time, and that Verdi himself was 'alive and well and still writing'.

Although he was only working as a hack writer for Ricordi, Boito had gradually grown out of his rash, idealistic phase to become a serious force in musical affairs. It was he who prepared the public so well for the Bologna production of *Lohengrin* that Wagner wrote him a public letter thanking him for the good reception it had received. As a member of Milan's City Council, Boito had been instrumental in persuading the members to pay for the first performance of Verdi's *Requiem* for Manzoni.

It is plainly obvious that a little conspiracy was hatched

Franz Liszt, born in 1811, 'the year of the comet', died in Bayreuth on 31 July 1886. Wagner's father-in-law, arguably the greatest pianist of the 19th century, and one of the most progressive composers and teachers of the day, Liszt was renowned for his operatic transcriptions and paraphrases. Among these were nine Verdi settings, beginning with the 'Salve Maria de Jérusalem' from *I Lombardi* (1848) and ending with the *Rémiscences de Boccanegra* published by Ricordi in 1883. Liszt also utilised material from *Ernani, Il trovatore, Rigoletto, Don Carlos, Aida* and the *Requiem*. Photograph by Nadar

behind Verdi's back. When he was in Milan during July 1879 to conduct a charity performance of the *Requiem* to assist the victims of the Po valley floods, Faccio and Ricordi went to dinner with the Verdis in their suite at the Grand Hotel. The conversation was steered round to the subject of Boito and *Othello.** Ricordi said later that 'at the mention of *Othello* I saw Verdi look hard at me, with suspicion, but with interest. He had certainly understood; he had certainly reacted. I believed the time was ripe'. In fact Verdi was persuaded to meet Boito the next day, and three days after that he presented Verdi with a scenario for the opera, which he surely must have worked on before the fateful dinner party. 'Write the libretto,' Verdi told him. 'It will come in handy for yourself, for me, or for someone else.'

* *Othello* as in Shakespeare; *Otello* as in Verdi.

137

Verdi in the late 1870s

Arrigo Boito (1842–1918)

So that the news of a possible new opera should not leak out, it was decided that it should be referred to as the 'chocolate project'. When Ricordi proposed bringing 'a friend' to Sant' Agata Verdi would have none of it. 'If you come now with Boito, I shall have to read his libretto. If I think it completely good, you will leave it with me, and I shall find myself, to a certain extent, committed.' Ricordi therefore visited him alone, but in spite of his continued refusal to give a firm undertaking to compose the opera, Verdi did begin to look at costumes and pictures in order to visualise the characters more clearly. Boito, hampered by toothache from an abscess, worked on the libretto (he called it 'manufacturing chocolate') throughout the summer, and was pleased that Verdi liked the part he showed him in the autumn. However the year slipped away quickly, and the New Year of 1880 found Verdi suggesting to the painter Domenico Morelli that he should do a sketch from *Othello* to match one he had done from *Lear*, of which he had sent Verdi a photograph. (The science of photography had been progressing rapidly in the second half of the century.)

Yet still the 'chocolate project' remained only an idea. In Milan on 18 April 1880 Verdi's settings of the *Pater Noster* and *Ave Maria* were first performed, but there was no real indication in the latter piece of the simple and beautiful prayer for Desdemona that was to follow. Giuseppina advised the conspirators to 'leave things, at least for the moment, just as they are, wrapping the Moor in as great a silence as possible.' So Ricordi returned to the idea he had first broached as long ago as 1868—a revision of *Simon Boccanegra*. He had tried to reopen the subject in 1879 but had had an unfavourable reply from Verdi on 2 May: 'I received yesterday a large parcel which I suppose to be a score of *Simon*. If you come to S.Agata six months, a year, two or three, etc. from now, you will find it untouched just as you sent it to me. I hate unnecessary things.' Now, a year later, Verdi capitulated and agreed to work with Boito on a revision.

In a recently discovered letter of 8 December 1880 Boito compared the opera in its original form to a rickety table of which only one leg, the Prologue, was sound. He also said that no character made one exclaim 'drawn from life!' He sent Verdi the outline of a completely new act, but the composer, though he admired the scheme, felt that it involved too much work. He replied on 11 December:

Having unfortunately to give up this act we must keep to the scene in the Council Chamber, which, I have no doubt, written by you

Franco Faccio (1840–91).
Caricature by Cima

Richard Wagner
(1813–83), Verdi's great
German contemporary.
It has been said that
whereas Verdi was
always primarily
concerned with *theme*

could not possibly be dull. Your criticisms are just, but you, immersed in loftier works and with *Otello* in mind, are aiming at a perfection impossible here. I aim lower and am more optimistic than you and don't despair. I agree that the table is rickety but if the legs are adjusted a bit I think it will stand up ... I agree that there are none of those characters (always very rare) that make one exclaim 'drawn from life!' Nevertheless it seems to me that there is something to be made of characters like Fiesco and Simone.

The refashioning took six weeks of complicated consultation which, if anything, made the plot more obscure. Verdi wrote to his friend Opprandino Arrivabene: 'Now if you really want to know, I'll tell you that I think *Boccanegra* will be able to go the rounds of the theatres like so many of its sisters even though the subject is a very sad one. It's sad because it has to be sad, but it's gripping.' This was not the only disadvantage he saw in the opera. In a letter to Ricordi in 2 December 1880 he wrote: 'In *Forza* the characters are ready-made; in *Boccanegra* you have to make them.' In other words, for a production of *Simon* to be successful the standard of acting has to be particularly high. There is no doubt that it has its flaws. Verdi was revising a work from the age of the *cabaletta* in the light of a new era in which the *cabaletta* was extinct and the act was the basic unit. When one takes into account also the complex and sombre plot with its preponderance of low male voices, one can see why *Simon Boccanegra* is not as immediately attractive as other late Verdi operas. The *première* on 24 March 1881 was conducted by Boito's friend Franco Faccio, who had now replaced Mariani as Italy's leading conductor. Among the principals were Maurel and Tamagno, soon to make their mark as the first Iago and Otello.

In the summer of 1880 Verdi had begun to correspond with Boito about the details of the *Otello* libretto, yet it still moved slowly and, as each Christmas came, Ricordi sent Verdi the gentle reminder of a cake with the figure of a Moor in chocolate icing on the top. At the end of 1882 and throughout the following year Verdi was occupied with the revision of *Don Carlos*, communicating with du Locle only through an intermediary. He had thought that the work would have to be shortened for a performance at the Vienna Opera but, when that fell through, it was given at La Scala in January 1884.

Meanwhile the passing years continued to take their toll. When Wagner died in 13 February 1883 in Venice, Verdi wrote to Giulio Ricordi: 'It is a great individual who has disappeared. A name that leaves the most powerful imprint on the history of art!' Then Carlo Tenca, Contessa Maffei's

*Continued from
previous page*
and harmony in his
musical technique,
Wagner was
preoccupied with the
contrasting notion of
harmony and theme, a
subtle but crucial
distinction

Milan, the Galleria
Vittorio Emanuele with
its iron and glass roof
and its gas lamps (Mary
Evans)

husband in all but name and editor of the literary magazine
Rivista Europea, died. Verdi admired her courage and told her
that he knew no words could bring comfort in such sorrow;
but Tenca's death caused him to comment: 'My years are
really beginning to be too many, and I think .... I think that
life is such a stupid thing, and, what is worse, a pointless thing.
What do we do? What shall we do? Taking it all together,
there is only one answer, humiliating, and extremely sad:
NOTHING!' Two great figures of Verdi's lifetime also died—
Garibaldi and Victor Hugo. Verdi's world was rapidly
changing, a speed of change that could be seen at the Milan
Industrial Fair of 1881. It was housed in the new Galleria
Vittorio Emanuele constructed of iron and glass and
illuminated by gas. One of the sights of the city was to watch
the little engine carrying a flame travel round inside the
circular dome to light the two thousand gas jets.

The advent of gas lighting had brought a great change to
the theatres. Previously they had been lit by candles so that the
house lights had remained on during performances, allowing

people to visit each other in their boxes (as Little Dorrit discovered at La Fenice), and thus operas were performed against a background of chatter. *Aida* was given with gas lighting; *Falstaff* by electricity (Edison invented the electric light bulb in 1879). This new lighting had an adverse effect on takings since, now the auditorium lights could be dimmed, talking during a performance was discouraged and the fashionable world gave up coming, but it did mean that audiences thereafter consisted mainly of music-lovers more ready to appreciate Verdi's final masterpieces.

The 'chocolate project' was very nearly abandoned altogether in the spring of 1884 when a newspaper reported Boito as saying that he was sorry he could not set *Otello* to music himself. Eventually he was able to persuade Verdi that he had been misquoted and that 'you alone can set *Otello* to music. All the dramatic creations you have given us proclaim this truth.' However the composer warned him that 'all this had led me to cool off somewhat on *Otello*, and has stiffened the hand that had begun to sketch a few bars'.

While Boito was engaged, amongst other things, in helping Puccini to find a theatre willing to stage his first opera *Le villi*, Verdi was concerned with more mundane matters including the financing and building of a twelve bed hospital at Villanova not far from Sant' Agata. He was closely involved at every stage with the design, construction, selection of staff and

Victor Maurel (1848–1923), the first Iago, and Verdi in the dressing room before the Paris *première* of *Otello*

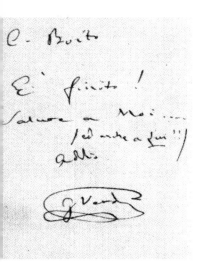

Verdi's famous note to Boito on the completion of *Otello*, 1 November 1886

furnishing, in which he enlisted Giuseppina's aid. When it was opened in 1887 he refused to let it be named after him so the façade still has the simple inscription *Ospedale*. This caused many to think of him as a limitless source of funds, so that he had to turn down ruthlessly suggestions that, for example, he should restore the church at Sant' Agata or contribute handsomely to Florence cathedral.

Still more of his friends died. Next to go was Giulio Carcano, translator of Shakespeare, who left Verdi his first edition of *I promessi sposi* inscribed by Manzoni. Shortly after the death of her former husband, Andrea, Contessa Maffei also died— of meningitis. Verdi rushed to her bedside but she was already unconscious. 'Poor Clarina! So kind, so considerate and so sensible. Oh, I shall certainly never forget her!' Verdi wrote to Antonio Ghislanzoni on 22 July 1886, four days after her death. 'We had been friends for forty-four years!! Poor Clarina!!' A little while later, just after Verdi had written him a cheery letter promising to visit him the next month, Arrivabene also died just before the *première* of *Otello*. One can only hope that the work on his opera cushioned for Verdi the loss of such old and dear friends.

He finished the composition in October 1885 but then revised and scored it during the next year, so that it was not until November 1886 that he wrote to Boito:

It's finished!
Greetings to us ... (and also to *him*!!)
Farewell.

The days of rapid composition and hurried orchestration were gone. Boito had proved an admirable librettist, willing to discuss, revise and rewrite; yet he was a skilful craftsman in his own right. His most important decision was to dispense with Shakespeare's first act during which Othello defends himself before the Venetian Senate and Brabantio. Instead the opera opens in great suspense with a storm at sea witnessed by the crowd as they await Otello's return as victor against the Turks. His 'Esultate' as he passes across the stage on landing is an amazingly brief first entrance for the main character, yet it at once establishes him as a man of authority and power, and is effectively contrasted with the love duet with Desdemona at the end of the act.

Another of Boito's important innovations was Iago's 'Credo' in which he expresses his philosophy of hatred, and shows himself as a man conceiving evil within himself which he knows he is destined to achieve. Again, by the beautifully

Francesco Tamagno (1851–1915) in the final scene of *Otello*

poignant 'Willow Song' and 'Ave Maria' that draw out the pathos while heightening the suspense, and by concentrating the final action into a fairly brief resolution Boito and Verdi created an ending of tragic, yet majestic, proportions.

'The dream has become a reality', wrote Boito, but now the opera had to be cast. Victor Maurel reminded Verdi that he had once promised him the part of Iago and, although inclined at first to demur, Verdi agreed. Maurel took the part most seriously as Muzio reported to Ricordi: 'He would even like to shave his beard, since he considers that a full beard makes his face too gentle .... In the second act he is playful, humorous, ironic, but from the 'Credo' onwards very terrible, and he says that the movement of his features needs to be clearly seen!' However Verdi was less certain about the choice of Francesco Tamagno for Otello, since he was not sure he could sing softly enough as he 'must always sing full voice, otherwise his tone becomes ugly and uncertain in pitch'. In the end Verdi coached him thoroughly, even showing him how to stab himself properly, rolling off the dais at rehearsal in spite of his seventy-four years! Tamagno and Maurel were both tremendous successes. Not so the Desdemona, one Romilda Pantaleoni, much loved and put forward for the part by Franco Faccio, who was to be the conductor. She was unable to convey the innocence and gentleness Verdi felt to be so essential to the part.

Nevertheless the *première* at La Scala on 5 February 1887 was an overwhelming triumph, in the words of Julian Budden—'one of the great events in Italy's history'. Verdi and Boito were applauded to the skies and at five in the morning crowds in the street were still shouting: 'Viva Verdi!' Although some

The *première* of *Otello* at La Scala

lamented the passing of the age of simpler music dramas, most hailed it as a masterpiece. Antonio Fogazzaro declared: 'From now on it will not be possible to set to music absurd music dramas and lamentable verses. Since this type of music follows faithfully the words, the words will have to be worthy of being followed.' The young Toscanini rushed home, dragged his mother out of bed and forced her to kneel on the floor and repeat 'Viva Verdi!'

Whether or not it is better than *Falstaff*, or better than Shakespeare's play, *Otello* remains the greatest Italian operatic tragedy. It probes the tumult of the human mind and its passions, its dark facets, and the beauty of existence. It is a supreme creation, distilled by the convergence of the genius of three men—Shakespeare, Boito and Verdi—and the wonder of it all is that it was not their final legacy to humanity.

Of course, everyone immediately urged Verdi to write another opera. The management of La Scala suggested a comedy based on *Don Quixote*. But he was not to be tempted and for two and a half years returned to his country life. He refused to go to Rome for the first production of *Otello* there, but instead supervised the completion of the hospital. Once it had been opened it needed his care and attention. He was much distressed to hear in January 1889 many complaints that the food and wine were inadequate, and that people who could not afford to pay were being charged for funerals. His threat to close the hospital soon put things right. It was certainly much needed in the area especially since poverty, hunger and illness increased during the government's tariff

144

Verdi in 1889

Giuseppina in 1890

war with France. Verdi was extremely concerned at the state of the country as he watched thousands emigrating. He did his best in his *paese* by reducing rents, reclaiming swamps near the Po for agriculture, building three new dairy farms to help unemployment, and introducing a new irrigation system.

In July 1889 Boito sent by post an outline for *Falstaff*. Verdi was immediately attracted by the idea, but replied:'As long as one wanders in the realm of ideas every prospect pleases, but when one comes down to earth, to practical matters, doubts and discouragements arise. In outlining *Falstaff* did you never think of the enormous number of my years?'

Boito replied by quoting the poet Foscolo's tag 'A smile adds a thread to the tapestry of life' and pressed Verdi to prove those people wrong who had said of *Otello*: 'It's impossible to.... finish better.' 'All your life you've wanted a good subject for a comic opera, and this is a sign that the vein of an art that is joyous in a noble way is virtually in existence in your brain.' Verdi replied: 'Amen, so be it! We'll write *Falstaff* then! We won't think for a moment of obstacles or age or illness.'

So Boito began work immediately and, though he found it difficult 'to extract the juice from the enormous Shakespearian orange without letting the useless pips slip into the little glass', he surpassed himself in his portrayal of Sir John in love. It is said that Elizabeth I had asked Shakespeare to write a play about Falstaff in love but had given him such a short time limit that the Bard had only been able to fill *The Merry Wives of Windsor* with stock characters. Boito imported many of Sir John's unique characteristics from the history plays to transform him into a spendidly alive creation.

Even Ricordi was not let into the secret for some time, while Verdi composed steadily, never for more than two hours a day to conserve his health. He altered amazingly little of Boito's text, setting most of it just as he received it. During this time he undertook few public commitments, agreeing only to become an honorary member of the Musical Society of the Beethoven-Haus in Bonn and to conduct in 1892 part of a concert at La Scala on the occasion of the centenary of Rossini's birth 'for the sake of the dead composers'. However when La Scala planned a jubilee revival of *Oberto* he refused to have anything to do with it, though he was flooded with congratulatory messages, including one from the King. Such celebration, however, was clouded by Muzio's death. His life had ended in unhappiness. His only child had died, his American wife had left him, and he died alone in a Paris hospital.

Verdi and Boito at Sant' Agata

The news of the impending *Falstaff* soon became public. The story was told of a dinner at the Grand Hotel in Milan during November 1890 at which Giuseppina proposed a toast beginning: 'I drink to the large belly', thereby causing acute embarrassment to Ricordi's married and pregnant daughter until Peppa added 'who is Falstaff'. On 3 December 1890 Verdi wrote an explanatory letter to Gino Monaldi, the art critic who was later to write a series of highly inaccurate 'recollections' of Verdi:

What can I tell you? For forty years now I have wanted to write a comic opera, and for fifty years I have known *The Merry Wives of Windsor*. However the usual 'buts' which pop up everywhere have always prevented me from doing what I wanted. Now Boito has swept away all the 'buts', and has written me a lyrical comedy which is unlike all others. I am enjoying myself writing the music. I have no plans for it, and I don't even know if I shall finish it ... I repeat, I'm enjoying myself ....

Certainly Verdi seems to have entered into the comic spirit of the entire venture, with the consequence that many of his and Boito's letters are highly amusing. For instance on 12 June 1891 he wrote to the librettist:

Old Paunchy is in a fair way to going mad. There are days when he doesn't move, but sleeps and is in a bad temper. At other times he shouts, runs, jumps, causes a devil of a rumpus. I let him indulge his whims a bit; if he goes on like this I'll put him in a muzzle and a straight-jacket.

To which Boito replied two days later:

Three cheers! Let him go, let him run; he will break all the windows and all the furniture of your room—no matter, you will buy some more. He will smash your piano—no matter you will buy another. Let everything be turned upside down so long as the great scene is finished. Three cheers. Go on! Go on! What pandemonium! But pandemonium as clear as sunlight and as dizzy as a madhouse!

When Faccio tragically suffered Donizetti's fate by going insane and then dying a year later in July 1891, Boito took over his job as Director of the Parma Conservatory for that year so that Faccio had a source of income. After his friend's death, Boito joined Verdi in conspiring to have Edoardo Mascheroni appointed to the vacant conductor's post at La Scala, which meant that he would direct the first production of *Falstaff*.

Twenty-five years later Toscanini discovered in the *Falstaff* manuscript the following inscription in Verdi's hand:

'Tutto è finito. Va, va, vecchio John. Cammina per la tua via fin che tu puoi. Divertente tipo di briccone eternamente vero sotto maschera diversa in ogni tempo, in ogni luogo. Va, va, cammina,

cammina, addio.' ('It's all finished. Go, go, old John. Go on your way for as long as you can. Amusing rogue, forever true beneath the masks you wear at different times and places. Go, go, carry on, carry on, farewell.')

Finished it may have been, but the *première* was jeopardised when Maurel, who was to sing the title rôle, began to demand excessive fees and a monopoly in the part. Verdi countered this by threatening to withdraw the opera from La Scala, which anyway he considered to be too big for the opera's intimate setting; but the matter was settled and rehearsals began. Even though he was in his eightieth year, Verdi attended rehearsals for up to eight hours a day, and also withstood a veritable bombardment from journalists, friends, well-wishers and *bores*. The *première* on 9 February 1893 was predictably another triumph, even though the performance was by no means perfect. After it Verdi and Boito only managed to escape from the theatre by a side door, and were then forced to appear several times on the hotel balcony until the cheering crowds dispersed. Verdi was similarly besieged when he went to Rome for the opening of *Falstaff* there, and had to be smuggled into a workmen's toolshed at the station to escape the milling throng. At the first night the King and Queen ushered him to the front of their box and then left him there alone to receive the plaudits of the audience.

Falstaff has given some the impression that Verdi's stream of melody had dried up. There are no set pieces that can be detached for separate performance, nor any recitative. A great many of the melodic phrases spring from the verbal rhythms and thus they pass by so quickly that the listener has difficulty in 'retaining' them in his head, and the opera is given its particular 'seamless' quality. Verdi had, like Wagner, learnt the art of transition, following his earlier works which are made up of contrasting blocks of music. No words can give any idea of the effect or structure of *Falstaff*. It cannot be described—it has to be experienced. Although there are flashes of humour in some of his other operas, Verdi had waited fifty-three years since his first attempt at comedy. Sir John's final words 'Tutto nel mondo è burla' (All the world's a jest') have often been taken as an epithet summing up Verdi's attitude to life. Perhaps it would be more accurate to take the last two lines of the opera sung by the chorus as a fitting comment upon *Falstaff*, the completion of Verdi's operatic outpouring:

'Ride ben chi ride la risata final' ('The best laugh of all is the one that comes last')

Maurel as the first Falstaff

Chapter 10
Requiem

'The sun of his Olympian old age'—Boito

After the *première* of *Falstaff*, Verdi had been appalled to hear that it was proposed to confer upon him the title of Marquis of Busseto, but he successfully appealed to the Minister of Education to prevent it. Nevertheless when he went to Paris in 1894 for a production of *Otello*, for which he had written a ballet, he was given no opportunity to refuse when the President of the Republic invited him into his box at the Opéra, informed him that he had been awarded the Grand Cross of the Légion d'Honneur and presented him to the audience. The festivities lasted for several days and included a memorial service for Gounod at which Verdi represented Italy, and a State banquet at the Elysée Palace where Giuseppina was also a guest of honour, which must have touched them both greatly. When Verdi had been honoured by the King of Italy in Rome, she had been ignored. His attitude to honours was not consistent. Later in 1900 he refused Italy's highest decoration that the King could offer him, the Collare dell'Annunziata, but accepted a similar award from the Austrian Emperor Franz Josef. Perhaps he felt that in Italy he could make his views plain, whereas abroad he would cause grave offence by turning down a proffered honour.

However, in the years after *Falstaff*, he had another project to occupy him. In 1889 he had bought some land outside Milan, on which he had intended to build a hospital and convalescent home, but his work on *Falstaff* had prevented further progress. After spending the winter in Genoa, Verdi and Giuseppina went to Milan in January 1895 to consult the architect Camillo Boito, Arrigo's elder brother. The plan was now to build a two storey rest home for one hundred retired musicians who at the end of their working lives had no pension to support them. Verdi involved himself in the plans at every stage. For example, he decided that there should not be dormitory accommodation, but rather rooms for two people so that they

The Casa di Riposa per Musicisti—the Musicians' Rest Home near Milan

could help each other in necessity, even though the enormous cost of providing two windows for every room prohibited his idea of giving complete privacy by a partition. Construction began in 1896 on the building he called 'my greatest work [opera]'. It was not completed until after his death, but in his will he left it the royalties from all his operas as well as a share in half his fortune (the hospital at Villanova and various charities in Genoa and Busseto were the other beneficiaries, with the remaining half and the Villa Verdi going to his adopted daughter Maria).

He was quite determined not to write his memoirs and told inquirers flatly that since 'the musical world has put up with my notes for so long a time, I shall never condemn it to read my prose'. Boito tried to tempt him to compose another opera by suggesting *Anthony and Cleopatra* or even *King Lear* once more, but, although he turned the ideas down, he continued to compose a little every day, declaring to Mascheroni: 'Every man has his destiny: one to be a donkey all his life, another to be a cuckold, one to be rich and another poor. As for myself, with my tongue in my mouth like a mad dog, I'm fated to work to the last gasp.'

He had always had a great admiration for Palestrina, so, when Boito asked him to suggest a composer after whom a proposed School of Choral Singing could be named, he mentioned Palestrina *in primis ante omnia* (first and before all others). In 1879 he had written a diatribe to Arrivabene against the 'Germanizing' of Italian music through the foundation of

149

innumerable Quartet and Orchestral Societies, and had concluded his letter: 'But if, instead, we Italians were to form a vocal quartet to perform Palestrina and his contemporaries, Marcello, etc., etc., wouldn't that, too, be "great art"? And it would be Italian art.' When the *Gazzetta Musicale* outlined an 'enigmatic scale', Boito asked Verdi why he did not write an *Ave Maria* incorporating it as a penance for the blasphemy of Iago's 'Credo'. Verdi retorted that Boito himself, having written the words of the 'Credo', was even more responsible and had better atone by writing a four-part 'Credo alla Palestrina' for *Nerone* (Boito's opera which he was never to complete). Verdi did, however, set an *Ave Maria* to the scale but disparagingly called the piece a 'charade'. At about the same time, in the years between *Otello* and *Falstaff*, he also composed a rather lovely *Laudi alla Vergine Maria* to words from Dante's *Paradiso*, and his setting certainly recalls Palestrina and sixteenth century polyphony. Now, in his last years, he wrote two further pieces. The first was a *Stabat Mater*, the medieval Latin poem describing Mary's grief as she stood at the foot of the cross. Verdi's setting is movingly expressive, capturing the deep sorrow of the mother weeping at the death of her son. The other piece was a *Te Deum*, the text of which dates from the fourth and fifth centuries. Before writing it, Verdi investigated how other composers had set it. The *Te Deum* is traditionally a paean of praise used to celebrate special occasions like victories and coronations, but Verdi realised that the text was more varied than that. His version is certainly less dramatic than his *Requiem*—its austere grandeur makes it one of the most impressively original of all settings of the canticle. It ends with a soprano solo proclaiming 'In thee, O Lord, have I trusted; let me never be confounded', after which there are six bars of orchestral music, his last published music, conveying once more the questing uncertainty so typical of him.

He had not conceived these four pieces as linked works, and indeed the two longer ones are for chorus and orchestra while the other two are for unaccompanied voices. However, they were eventually published together in 1898 when Boito arranged a *première* in Paris during Holy Week, although Verdi would not allow the *Ave Maria*, the slightest of the pieces, to be given. The *Quattro Pezzi Sacri* (*Four Sacred Pieces*) are now usually given together and, although at the first performance it was the *Laudi* that received most acclamation, the *Te Deum* has received just recognition as one of its composer's finest works.

Verdi's good health continued to amaze everyone until, in

Verdi reflecting on his memories in the park he created at Sant' Agata. A photograph

January 1897, Peppina found him lying in bed one morning in their apartment at the Palazzo Doria in Genoa motionless and unable to speak. While she conferred with Maria Carrara as to whether they should call a doctor, Verdi wrote in a shaky hand 'Caffè'. After he had been given some, he recovered, so the incident was kept a secret from all but a few. Indeed a friend who saw the Verdis at Montecatini in the following July wrote:

She walks with difficulty, all bent over and supporting herself on his arm. He, on the other hand, what vigour he still has for his eighty-four years [he was actually eighty-three]. He has a cloud of white hair which, joined with his beard, forms a sort of halo. He holds himself straight, walks briskly, and turns easily; he talks quickly and can remember facts, dates and names, and set forth his ideas on art clearly.

Soon after they returned to Sant' Agata, Giuseppina was in bed for several weeks with bronchitis, and although she recovered, she continued to cough and ate little. Just before they were to leave to spend the winter in Genoa she developed pneumonia and lay in bed for three days without fever or pain. When Verdi brought her a flower, she apologized for being unable to smell it. At four o'clock in the afternoon of 14 November 1897, with Verdi beside her, she died. She was eighty-two. At her request her funeral was a simple one in Busseto with no flowers or music, but with many local people and friends, including Teresa Stolz and Ricordi.

Verdi was desolate. He wrote to a friend: 'Great grief does not demand great expression; it asks for silence, isolation, I would even say the torture of reflection. There is something superficial about all exteriorization; it is a profanation.' Giuseppina had been absolutely the right person for Verdi, loving him deeply as a man, appreciating his talents as an artist. She stood beside him rather than trying to influence or direct him, but she sometimes conspired to start him on the creative process even though this meant that she effectively 'lost' him for many months. She was able to live through his moods of depression, and she dealt magnificently with the potentially disastrous relationship with Teresa Stolz. She had always been a devout Catholic and it was a continual source of regret to her that Verdi, though ready to build a chapel in Sant' Agata and write the *Requiem* and other sacred pieces, was not able to subscribe formally to the faith she held so dear. Above all she accepted him as the 'bear' he often was, and compensated as much as possible for his times of ill-nature by showing to others her own kinder, more sympathetic and

Verdi at Montecatini, 1898, with various friends including Teresa Stolz sitting next to him. A photograph (Julian Budden)

generous nature. Her will ended: 'Now, *addio, mio Verdi*. As we were united in life, may God rejoin our spirits in Heaven.'

Verdi's grief was perhaps the cause of a weakening of his physical powers; his eyesight was failing, his hand trembled and his legs would not support him. He wrote to Mascheroni a little while later: 'I am not sick but I am too old! Think of spending your life without being able to do anything! It is very hard.' It must have been particularly difficult for him, since he was used to working out his moods of depression by activity on his estate.

Although death had taken away so many, he was still visited regularly by several friends including Stolz, Ricordi and Boito. He continued to negotiate with lawyers to establish the *Casa di Riposa* (the Musicians' Rest Home) as a charitable foundation, but he found Sant' Agata lonely now, so spent more time at the Grand Hotel, Milan, where Maria Carrara-Verdi had a room in his suite in which she often stayed. Friends came almost every night to dinner and to while away the night in conversation. A series of minor heart attacks prevented him going to Paris for the *première* of the *Quattro Pezzi Sacri*. This was such a success that an Italian *première* was given in Turin with Toscanini conducting.

During the 1890s Verdi had been depressed by further political tangles in Italy which reached the height of stupidity

Over page
Facsimile of a letter dated 21 May 1898 and written by Verdi to Alessandro Bonci (1872–1942). Bonci as a young tenor had sung the part of Riccardo in *Un ballo in maschera* at Florence and had introduced the rhythmical laughs in the rests during the Act I quintet 'E scherzo od è follia' that have been copied by many tenors since. In this letter Verdi says what a pleasant surprise this 'unique innovation' has been to him 'and it made me laugh inside taking me back to the far-off days when I wrote it'. He tells Bonci that 'it confirms to me your skill and the care you put into every performance', so that, when other lesser singers like Casini 'fade away', Bonci will not. Verdi then points out that, although his librettist Antonio Somma wrote marvellous lines like Riccardo's famous aria 'Eri tu', (Verdi) has some pangs of regret when playing the score over on the piano which he did not notice before and particularly at the sentence 'Sento l'orma

when the Prime Minister, Francesco Crispi, tried to imitate the French and British moves into North Africa by an invasion of Ethiopia which ended in the massacre of the Italian army at Adowa. Italy seethed with unrest until King Umberto, good-natured though he was but too identified with the forces of reaction, was shot by an anarchist in July 1900. The Queen wrote a prayer that was published in the newspapers. Several people suggested to Verdi that he should set it to music, but he declined on the grounds of ill health and old age. Nevertheless he did sketch out several bars, but it remained unfinished. With the ascent of Vittorio Emanuele III to the throne, a liaison between the monarchy and the moderate Left was established and a period of advancing prosperity began that was to last until the Great War. The seeds of the Risorgimento were beginning to flower.

By the time he was eighty-seven in October 1900 everything tired Verdi. 'Why am I still in this world?' he mused. As he could not walk far, he had to be wheeled round the park at Sant' Agata. In December he went to the Grand Hotel in Milan once more and spent Christmas there with Maria, Stolz, Boito, Ricordi and his family. Teresa Stolz wrote to Maria Waldmann, now a grandmother:

Our beloved Maestro is well, despite his eighty-seven years. He enjoys a good appetite, sleeps well, often goes out for drives, sometimes walks a little, but complains of his legs, saying he would take longer walks but his legs are weak. For the rest he is in good humour, likes company and every evening has a gathering of his most intimate friends at his lodgings. Later on, in March, he will leave for Genoa.

It was not to be. On 21 January 1901 as he was sitting on his bed buttoning his waistcoat, he had a stroke, falling back on to the bed unconscious. He survived for several days, during which the hotel was draped in black, straw was put down in the streets to muffle the sound of carriage wheels, while his friends inside, and crowds outside, watched and waited. He died without regaining consciousness at ten minutes to three on the morning of 27 January 1901. Boito later wrote to a friend:

He died magnificently, like a fighter, formidable and mute. The silence of death had fallen over him a week before he died .... His resistance was heroic. The breathing of his great chest sustained him for four days and three nights. On the fourth night the sound of his breathing still filled the room, but the fatigue .... Poor Maestro, how brave and handsome he was, up to the last moment!

My dear friend, in the course of my life I have lost those I have idolized, and grief has outlasted resignation. But never have I

Milano il 21 Maggio 1897 —

Al bravo tenore Bonci
Grand Hôtel Savoia
Firenze

Caro Bonci:

Nel nostro Veneziano Ballo in Maschera che il pubblico fiorentino predilige la Vostra interpretazione mi è stata una sorpresa graditissima e mi ha fatto ridere; ridere col pensiero, tornando col tempo lontano in cui lo scrissi —

... È scherzo od è follia ....

Vo detto quasi parlato e spiccato col canto e l'aggiunta della risata rispettando il tempo e gli [illegible]

"È" una Vostra unica [illegible] e specialità" che Vi riconosco e che mi conferma la Vostra perizia e lo studio che Voi ponete in ogni esecuzione.

"Grazie a mio pensiero [illegible]!"

Anche [illegible] nei [illegible] molto mi [illegible] e [illegible] [illegible] dopo di cantare!!

... E risentendo Voi e lui nei rispettivi ruoli il contrasto è così vero che invidio i Vostri [illegible] [illegible] — Voi giocondo peccatore!

Il mio librettista aveva scritto:

Eri tu che macchiavi quell'anima! mia ... quell'angelo! e non ho che un [illegible] rimorso quando prendo a uso il Verbo [illegible] e me lo rigiro a pianoforte di non aver notato prima la frase.

Santo l'orrore dei [illegible] [illegible]!!

.. Ma i fiorentini mordacissimi lo notarono subito.... Del resto ben [illegible] libretti di strafalloni non ne mancano! E in generale noi musicisti (salvo Boito [illegible] e il mio grande rivale Wagner) siamo tutti poco ignari del verso e ben incuranti del significato letterale.

Mi accorgo di aver divagato attorno a Voi:

La vecchiaia mi pesa, ma non mi toglie di tanto in tanto il buon umore. Se a Settembre venite a Montecatini mi ci troverete come sempre e forse avrò bisogno di Voi per [illegible] una nuova [illegible] (un po' [illegible]) ....

Non fate troppo lo [illegible] con le donne .... [illegible]!

State in pace. È vero che [illegible] ancora a [illegible] giorno [illegible]

.... la [illegible] ... Ecco una gran Verità!

Tanti, tanti saluti Vostro

G. Verdi

Grazie dei vostri auguri e della Vostra lettera che [illegible] la mia vista [illegible] [illegible] ... [illegible]...

dei passi spietati' ('I hear their pitiless step advancing') at which the Florentine audience had obviously laughed. 'On the other hand', Verdi continues, 'in my old libretti there were plenty of bits of nonsense. In general we musicians (except Boito, Leoncavallo *and my great rival Wagner*) are not all very good at versifying and not very scrupulous about the literal meaning of the words.' Verdi then says that although 'old age lies heavy on me, that does not deprive me of occasional good humour', so he suggests that Bonci comes in September to Montecatini where he will find him as usual and where he will be able to cheer him up by performing the laugh for him. The letter ends with an admonition not to chase after women 'especially those of the Theatre! Be moderate! It is true that you are still very young! But … moderation is a great virtue!' (Professor Olga Bonci, Scuola di Bel Canto, Bologna; photograph by courtesy of Maria Giovanna Muszynska, London)

experienced such a feeling of hatred against death, of contempt for that mysterious, blind, stupid, triumphant and craven power. It needed the death of this octogenarian to arouse those feelings in me.

Although a splendid public funeral had been prepared, this had to be altered when it became known that his will requested that it should be 'very modest, either at dawn or at the time of the *Ave Maria* in the evening, and without music and singing'. So his coffin was borne on a hearse preceded by a single crucifix to the cemetery where he was to lie beside Peppina, but the crowd, even at half past six on a damp, foggy morning, softly sang the 'Va, pensiero' chorus.

His will had requested that he be buried with Peppina in the oratory in the *Casa di Riposa,* so, when the building was completed, there was another funeral as the coffins were moved. Two hundred thousand people lined the streets of Milan; at the cemetery gates Toscanini conducted a choir of eight hundred in the *Nabucco* chorus; and Princes of Italy's royal House, leading politicians and important figures from many branches of Italian life walked behind the coffin with representatives from every region of the country.

Verdi's life had spanned a world of almost incredible change. His music, though part of his country's history, is also part of human experience for it reflects the deepest and yet the simplest human emotions. During his lifetime, and since his death, countless thousands have discovered in that music something of themselves; but the man who composed it continues partially to elude those who seek to find him. Sir Isaiah Berlin summed it up in these words:

Among composers of genius, Verdi is perhaps the last complete, self-fulfilled creator, absorbed in his art; at one with it; seeking to use it for no ulterior purpose, the god wholly concealed by his works, severe, farouche … suspicious of anyone curious about his inner life, wholly, even grimly, impersonal, drily objective, at one with his music. A man who dissolved everything in his art.

Verdi on his deathbed

The Maestro in 1899.

The second funeral
procession in the
Piazzale Cairoli, Milan.
L'Illustrazione Italiana, 3
February 1901 (Julian
Budden)

Index

158

2/94 (17249)